UP-HELLY-AA AND TAR-BARRELS

MADE AND PRINTED
IN GREAT BRITAIN
BY T. & J. MANSON
"SHETLAND NEWS"
OFFICE, LERWICK
SHETLAND

COLOUR FRONTISPIECE
BY HOOD & CO. LTD.
MIDDLESBROUGH

FACSIMILE EDITION
REPRINTED IN 2015
BY SHETLAND
HERITAGE
PUBLICATIONS

REPRODUCED BY
KIND PERMISSION
OF MRS MARJORY
HOGG
(née MITCHELL)

UP-HELLY-AA

TAR-BARRELS

AND

GUIZING

- LOOKING BACK -

BY

C. E. MITCHELL

T. & J. MANSON
"SHETLAND NEWS" OFFICE
LERWICK SHETLAND
1948

ISBN 978-0-9572031-6-7

Published by Shetland Heritage Publications, 2015.
Shetland Heritage Publications, Shetland Amenity Trust,
Garthspool, Lerwick ZE1 0NY.

PRINTED BY
THE SHETLAND TIMES
Gremista, Lerwick
Shetland ZE1 0PX

PREFACE.

WHY is it that no native-born Shetlander has ever written a history of the Tar-barrels and Up-Helly-Aa ? I think the answer is that, like getting up in the morning and going to bed at night, Tar-barrels and Up-Helly-Aa were part and parcel of Lerwegian life, and 'what was there to write about anyway?' : it is not much good telling people what they know already. Why ! In the Nineties, these celebrations were not thought worth more than an eight line paragraph in the local Press.

It was in the Eighties that, each summer, my father took to Lerwick his whole household—mother and family of six, an aunt, maids, "Fly" the cob and the phaeton, "Caesar" the Newfoundland dog and "Topsy" the Yorkshire terrier of uncertain lineage. These were the most glorious summers of our very youthful days.

It was during this period that I first heard of a mysterious affair, called a Tar-barrel, which made its appearance about Christmas-time. That the Tar-barrel had been suppressed for some years made no difference to the tales which gripped my imagination, and, long after my annual holidays had given place to permanent residence in Shetland, Tar-barrels, Up-Helly-Aa and the Yule festivities generally, maintained their interest for me. I took part in the Guizing and First Fittin' —mostly as a silent member, for no Southerner can hope to acquire the subtle cadence of the Shetlander's speech : might

just as well expect that a Cockney could pass himself off as a
'Buchan loon' in East Aberdeenshire.

The years passed, and the Fates ordained that I should
marry the niece of probably the last of the genuine old Tar-
barrellers, and from him I learnt all that was to be known of Tar-
barrelling days. I used to listen to his tales, and, purely as a
matter of personal interest, I began to write them down, and, later,
when I was persuaded to put them into more permanent form,
I decided to widen my subject and take in the whole Jola Bød
period and any matters of interest which took place about that
season. Naturally, I turned to the local Press, only to find that
all the early office files of the *Shetland Times* had been destroyed
by fire. Fortunately, with the exception of the first half-year of
publication, 1873, there were copies in the British Museum. I
have drawn my data largely from these early files, and, later,
also from both the *Shetland Times* and the *Shetland News*.
To the proprietors of both these papers, I tender my thanks for
their courtesy in allowing me to consult the files and to make
extracts from them.

I am also indebted to Mr James Goodlad of Goodlad &
Goodlad—the undischarged Special Constable—the late Mr
Ratter, Librarian, the late Mr William W. Ratter, retired
Public Assistance Officer, Mr E. S. Reid Tait, F.S.A.
(SCOT.), F.R.S.G.S., Mr P. Bruce Laurenson, L.D.S.,
Secretary to the Up-Helly-Aa Committee, for reminiscences
and information; and Mr John H. Spence, M.A., LL.B., for
reading proofs.

I am more especially indebted to Mr Tom Henry, whose
artistic skill is portrayed in the design of the cover and in the
black and white sketches which illustrate this volume, and to
Miss Dorothy Johnson, D.A., whom I commissioned to paint
the frontispiece which, I am sure, will arouse nostalgic longings
in the breasts of all exiled Shetlanders as they gaze on the Up-

Helly-Aa Torchlight Procession wending its way along the Hillhead and doon da Toon Hall Brae.

When the late Sir John Watson, Sheriff Principal, paid his last visit to Shetland, I gave him the draft of this book to read, and the following day he spent his last evening in Shetland sitting in my kitchen yarning—we had no maids and only one fire! When we came to discuss my efforts, the following conversation took place :—

Sir John.—Do you intend to publish your work ?

Myself.—I have not yet decided anything ; I wrote it for my own amusement and to give my friends a glimpse of Tar-barrels and Guizing.

Sir John.—Just so ! But if you decide to publish, will it be for Shetland readers or for readers in general ?

Myself.—Don't know ; I haven't even thought about it.

Sir John.—Well, if it is intended for Shetland readers, I would not alter a word, but, if it is intended for general reading, then I would cut out a whole lot of that early *Times* stuff ; too sententious and boring to anyone not a Shetlander.

Well, I have published it without cutting anything out, so the 'general reader' is warned to skip most of the extracts from the *Shetland Times.*

Sir John also insisted that I should write a short treatise on the Vikings, as very few people knew anything about them, and that it would add to the interest if people knew from what sort of folk the tradition of the Tar-barrels came. I have complied with his wishes, and in so doing have myself learnt who the Vikings were. Like the majority of people my knowledge of them was somewhat meagre. I borrowed from Mr E. S. Reid Tait two books on the subject, "The Vikings" by Professor Mawer, and "Northern Mythology" by Kaufmann, and from these and other sources I have written a short treatise which appears in Appendix V. I cannot claim to have given more than a sketchy account of the Vikings, but what I have written may encourage others to dip into what is one of the most important periods in the history of Europe.

Sir John would have written a Foreword, but within a few weeks he died on the train between London and Edinburgh, another victim of overstrain due to the war.

In conclusion, let me touch on a small personal incident. One night I was wading through the early extracts from the *Shetland Times*, and the children were making a distracting row. As I looked up with a reproving glance, I heard the small voice of my youngest daughter—"Sssh! Be quiet! Daddy is busy with his 'authorisation' ". I do not claim to be an author, so, if my 'authorisation' has failed, I hope that, at any rate, I have preserved a chapter in Shetland life which, otherwise, would have been lost.

C. E. MITCHELL.

Seafield,
    by Lerwick.

December, 1946.

CONTENTS.

LIST OF ILLUSTRATIONS.

INTRODUCTION.

L ITTLE seems to be known about the origin of Up-Helly-Aa. The actual meaning of the name is also obscure, but if we assume that the middle portion 'Helly'[1] has the same meaning as understood by Shetlanders of the present day, that is, the holy time or Sabbath, it is almost certain that Up-Helly-Aa had some connection with a pagan religious festival.

The late Sheriff Shennan, in his book "A Judicial Maid-Of-All-Work", mentions that "the word 'Uphaliday' is the name found in the 16th century applied to the feast of the Epiphany, 6th January, when the holiday time was ended". Although Up-Helly-Aa and Uphaliday refer to such widely different festivals, nevertheless they appear to be of common origin, and it will be a matter of interest to speculate on how the name of a pagan festival came to be applied to a Christian rite.

It is a matter of history that the early Christian teachers found that it simplified their missionary efforts to retain a pagan custom or rite, and to superimpose on it one appertaining to the new Christian faith. One of the best examples of this, was the superimposition of Christmas on pagan Yule. Did the same thing happen to the feast of the Epiphany? Up-Helly-Aa and Uphaliday are strangely alike in form and sound.

---

[1] A Shetlander speaks of going away 'over the Helly' in the same way as one would speak of going away for the week-end.

A

Each signifies the end of the holidays, and both festivals were celebrated in the month of January.

To pursue this interesting theme a little longer, we find further parallels between the two festivals. The feast of the Epiphany celebrates the manifestation of Christ to the Wise Men of the East, but the word 'Epiphany', itself, is purely pagan, and denoted the manifestation of a god or an emperor to his people. When Gaius Caesar, a grandson of Augustus, visited the island of Cos, his visit was recorded in a stone inscription which runs "In the first year of the epiphany of Gaius Caesar".

Now, when in the far north after his long winter sleep, the Sun-god revealed himself to his subjects, they celebrated his return in the burning of the Yule log and in general rejoicings. These rejoicings terminated with Up-Helly-Aa, and it is possible that the term 'Up-Helly-Aa' came to be associated as much with the manifestation of the Sun-god as with its more proper meaning—the last day of the festivities.

Just as the early Christians adopted the pagan designation 'Epiphany', and applied it to one of their own festivals, so, as time went on and the new faith spread northwards, the monks and the Norse converts would have to carry out the same tactics as those of the earlier teachers by adapting the existing pagan rites to the tenets of the new creed. Is it not, therefore, feasible to conclude that the Feast of the Epiphany was superimposed on Up-Helly-Aa or Uphaliday, and that, while the feast took on a new meaning, the old title 'Uphaliday' remained?

So much for speculation aroused by the mention of the Uphaliday of the Middle Ages but, leaving the realms of speculation, it is sufficient to know that Up-Helly-Aa is the final day of the Jola Bød or Yule Period which commenced on the fifth day of January, old style, and ended twenty-four days later in a climax of revelry and feasting.

At the end of the Jola Bød, MID-WINTER, the principal of the three great Norse sacrificial feasts, was celebrated, the other two being held in October and April. At this feast, for three days, the assembled people celebrated the Yuletide festival with feasting and drinking, and offering sacrifices to the gods.

When low down on the southern horizon the Sun-god lifted his flaming face, giving promise of light and warmth, the people hailed him with joy, not unmixed with fear, as they acclaimed his glory, and did obeisance to him. Did he gaze upon them in peace or in anger? They knew not; so the sacrificial fires on the altars were stirred to fiercer flames as the sacrifices of sheep and oxen were offered in the hope that the god would accept them and grant the offerers his favour, or, at worst, turn away his wrath.

Down through the ages, the tradition of the sacrificial fires has been passed from generation to generation. Two of the festivals have fallen by the way-side, but the greatest has defied oblivion, and now culminates in the world-famous celebration of Up-Helly-Aa which is held in Lerwick on the last Tuesday of January, each year.

The years are passing and, although the present day celebrations have eclipsed the days of the Tar-barrels, it may interest the youth of to-day to hear something of the manner in which the youth of yesterday carried on the tradition of their pagan forefathers.

CHAPTER I.

MOST of the genuine old Tar-barrellers have passed over to Valhalla, but it is to one of these stalwarts, the late Peter Garriock, for long Burgh Treasurer of Lerwick, that we are indebted for much of the detail and information which appear in these pages. Mr Garriock died in 1939 in his eighty-second year, and he used to relate how, in his early childhood, from a bedroom window in his father's house in Commercial Street, he first viewed the smoky, lurid flames of a Tar-barrel as it was hauled along the street by a number of wild, yelling, weirdly dressed figures who, to his childish mind, appeared to be demons enveloped in smoke and flames.

At this stage it is as well to explain that 'Tar-barrel' was the name given to the complete contraption of a wooden sledge on the top of which was a varying number of tubs filled with combustibles mixed with tar. A detailed description of a Tar-barrel will be given later.

Some years later, an old friend of Mr Garriock's father came home after a long exile in foreign parts and, as old cronies will, they used to spend whole evenings together going over old times. On such nights, school lessons were forgotten and it was a very discreet, attentive youngster who sat enthralled listening to tales of Greenland ships and of fights among their crews ashore, of Dutch busses and of smuggling, of guizing and of Tar-barrels in the days of their boyhood. The mind of youth is retentive and these reminiscences, together with many interesting details of the doings of a former generation, remained vivid in his mind, but it is the tales of the Tar-barrels and of the Yule festivities that claim our attention. Before retelling some of these, it is necessary to introduce the Special Constables, without whom most of the tales would lose their savour.

What would the citizens of Lerwick think if, to-day, the heads of households were called upon to present themselves to be sworn-in as special constables for duty during the Christmas festivities? Yet, that was a liability they had to face almost up to the end of last century. The authorities exercised their right to call on every householder for police duties, and insisted that, if for any reason he claimed exemption, he must produce a substitute. It is rather amazing to find that we have still with us a special constable who has never been officially released from duty. He is Mr James M. Goodlad of Messrs Goodlad & Goodlad. He relates that he was one of the 'suspect trouble makers' whom "Old MacKay" swore-in and forgot to release.

How many were called out depended on circumstances, but during his tenure of office, Chief Constable MacKay adopted a plan which went far to reduce his worries during the festive season. A few days before Yule, he would call upon such young men as he suspected might give him trouble, and inform them that they must report for special constable duty. Whether he acted *ultra vires* is beyond the point : Chief Constable MacKay had a way with him that few young men in Lerwick would have cared to dispute.

Just before the festivities commenced, the Specials were assembled in an upper room in the Tolbooth (now the premises of the Royal National Mission to Deep Sea Fishermen) and were duly sworn-in. This room was their place of assembly

and, when on duty, an ample supply of refreshments was kept
on hand.   It is said that the Specials did not always keep
these good things to themselves but would, on occasion, smuggle
some out to refresh the palates of their friends.

It is interesting to note that, at least up to the middle of
last century, loaded pistols were served out to the Specials.
Mr Garriock's father, who had, on several occasions, been
called upon to serve, used to relate that he and other Specials
would take the first opportunity to fire off their loaded pistols in
the seclusion of one of the lanes : loaded pistols in
the hands of men unversed in the ways of arms, were un-
chancy things, and the sooner they were made safe the better.

There are no records of the pistols ever having been used
in the discharge of duty, and it is more than likely that their
issue was a routine order dating back to the days when hostile
raids on the town were by no means improbable.   To illustrate
how obsolete orders can remain uncancelled, it will come as a
surprise to most people to hear that, on the outbreak of the
Great War, there was still in force an order that, on the
declaration of war, all officers' swords must be sharpened, and
it is a fact that at least six beautifully engraved, silverplated
swords, belonging to the officers of the Territorial Force in
Lerwick, suffered untold indignities on a grindstone at the hands
of a local joiner.

The authorities did not see eye to eye with the custom of
dragging blazing Tar-barrels through the town and, in addition
to keeping the peace, the special constables had standing orders
to seize all Tar-barrels and drag them over the banks[2] on to
the beach or tip them into the sea.   A state of war, therefore,
continued between the Tar-barrellers and the constables, with
the wits of the former ever on the alert to outwit the minions of
the law.

Having introduced the Specials, we can now proceed with

---

[2]Banks :—The first rising ground or rock above high-water mark.

retelling the tales which have been handed down. Like most one-sided histories, they record only victories, but doubtless, if records were available, it would be found that the authorities had more than their share of triumphs.

On one occasion, a squad[3] who, as we would say to-day, 'were well known to the police', had planned to burn their Tar-barrel on Yule morning, and had assembled all the necessary material for its construction, when information was brought to them that there was a large force of constables assembled in the Tolbooth. In the face of this news, to go on with their plans was to court disaster, as no sooner would their blazing Tar-barrel start on its journey through the Street[4] than word would be sent to the Tolbooth : the Tar-barrel would be seized and ignominiously thrown over the banks. To take all the materials back to the various places of concealment was unthinkable, so a Council of War was held to discuss ways and means of circumventing the Specials.

One member of the squad suggested that the Tar-barrel should not be set on fire until the Street was reached and then rushed through before the Specials had time to descend on them. As this was a departure from time-honoured custom, the suggestion was turned down. 'Either ablaze all the way or not at all' was the verdict.

Plan after plan was discussed but none seemed to give much hope of the Tar-barrel being able to run the gauntlet safely.

"What düs du suggest, Tammie?" This to the leader of the squad who, up till then, had not entered much into the discussions. "A'm tinkin', boys, ye hed better start an' pit her tagidder" was the laconic reply. In Tammie's brain

---

[3]Squad :—A self contained band of Guizers or Tar-barre'lers.
[4]The Street :—In Lerwick, Commercial Street is generally known simply as "The Street". Even to-day, a Lerwegian speaks of 'going to the Street' or says 'I met so-and-so on the Street'. All very confusing to the stranger who inevitably asks "But which street?". So throughout this narrative, Commercial Street will be mostly known as "The Street".

a plan was evolving which, for sheer audacity, would take
some beating.   While the construction of the Tar-barrel proceeded apace, Tammie detached two of the squad and sent
them off to fetch more materials from which a small Tar-barrel
was made.   This done, the smaller Tar-barrel was carried
along the Hillhead and taken quietly down Church Lane which
terminated just opposite the Tolbooth.

On reaching the bottom of the lane and making sure
that the coast was clear, Tammie had the Tar-barrel hoisted
on to his head and shoulders, carried it across the street and up
the steps of the Tolbooth, where he dumped it on the broad
flagstone in front of the doorway.   Having accomplished this,
he lost no time in closing the double doors and tying the handles
together.   For at least a brief space of time, interference from
inside could be ignored.   With flint and steel, Tammie ignited
a piece of tinder, fanned it into a flame and set the Tar-barrel
alight.   Waiting just long enough to ensure 'that it was well
ablaze, he hurried across the street and rejoined the squad.

It is not related what the feelings of the constables were,
when they discovered the trick that had been played on them.
The Tolbooth was not only the police headquarters, but was
also the town prison, and, as such, all windows were stoutly
barred.   The only means of escape was by the door, and, by
the time they had got this opened, the Tar-barrel was a roaring
furnace which effectively barred their exit.   No doubt, most
of the constables could have jumped through the flames, but
running tar on smooth steps was not the best of footholds : in
any case, the Specials did not feel called upon to give an
exhibition of fire-walking or, rather, jumping.   There was no
real danger of the building being set on fire.   It was comparatively easy to prevent the flames from igniting the plastered
walls inside the doorway.   There was nothing for it but to
accept the situation and remain 'prisoners of war' until the
furnace had burned itself out.

Meantime, the squad had returned to their main Tar-
barrel, and, having set it alight, hauled it in triumph over its
appointed course.

Tammie, the leader of this squad, was a youth named
Thomas Hughson, who, it is said, was a veritable Samson in
his day. The story is handed down, that Tammie was the last
man to do penance on the treadmill in Lerwick. The 'last
man', because he objected strongly to this form of hard labour
and, long ere he had done his spell on the mill, there was little
of it left for future offenders to tread. Whether this be a
legend or actual fact cannot be verified. The old stocks are
still in existence though nothing is known about the treadmill.

Tammie was an old offender who, in a long list of
offences, had included the use, or rather misuse, of gunpowder.
The authorities had, therefore, issued an order to the local
merchants, that, on no consideration, was he to be supplied
with any. In the days of our grandfathers, however, the
making of gunpowder was almost a home industry and, if
Tammie was debarred from buying it, there was no reason why
he should not make it : charcoal was simple to make, while
saltpetre and sulphur were household commodities. The
festive season was approaching and the festive season, without
crackers or 'cannons', as the larger sizes of squibs were called,
did not appeal to Tammie : he made his own.

Crackers were made by taking a small quantity of powder
and a strip of match[5], and rolling them tightly in thick paper
which was pasted between the layers. A convenient length
of match was left protruding from one end. One cracker he
made, which looked like the father of all crackers : in fact, it
was more like a bomb than anything else, and there was never
a doubt in his mind as to what he was going to do with it. It
was to be a present to Charles Gilbert Duncan, Writer,

---

[5]Match:—Fuse. The simplest form was made by soaking soft brown
paper in a solution of saltpetre and allowing it to dry.

Procurator Fiscal, to whose machinations Tammie ascribed the 'interdict' on his right to buy gunpowder for his 'harmless ploys'.

Choosing a suitable night, he proceeded to the house of the Fiscal to deliver his present. To ring the bell and hand it in with 'the season's compliments' would, no doubt, have been the correct procedure, but adherence to such polite etiquette was outwith Tammie's idea of the fitness of things. He had planned that the presentation should be made in a different manner : the Fiscal must be at home to receive his gift.

This was not quite so easy, for although the Fiscal's sitting room was on the ground floor, the inside window shutters were closed and only a small chink of light indicated that the room might be occupied. Tammie waited and listened. At last a sound, which he recognised, came from within the room. The Fiscal had coughed, and Tammie had heard that cough many times before during his frequent attendances in court. Pulling from under his jacket a harmless-looking brown paper parcel, he laid it on the sill of the window, produced his flint and steel and lit the fuse. Tammie retired to a strategic spot from which he could observe results.

The sizzling point of light gradually got nearer and nearer to the cracker and then it disappeared. Tammie knew quite well that it would take some little time for the spark to reach the powder, but, in his present state of nervous tension, he felt sure that the match had gone out. During these moments of suspense, he kept debating with himself as to whether he should or should not run back and retrieve his cracker. In fact, he had already taken a few cautious steps towards the window, when bang went the cracker, and it was a bang far beyond his most fervent expectations. There was a crash followed by the tinkling of falling glass and the shutters inside suddenly swung back, letting out a flood of light. Tammie did not wait for an acknowledgment of his Yule gift.

The following amusing tale relates to another triumph by the Tar-barrellers over the Specials.

On this occasion, it was known that the Specials were out in force and that there was little chance of a Tar-barrel proceeding far on its journey, so, once again, a squad took counsel together as to the best way of outwitting the law.

The orthodox method of dragging a Tar-barrel was by means of a heavy chain which was attached to the fore-end of the sledge. The chain was ideal for the purpose, but it had one great disadvantage in that, if the constables once got possession of the chain, the Tar-barrel's progress came to an abrupt end.

It was to over-come this drawback that the brains of the squad were directed, and after rejecting a number of suggestions, the following plan was adopted. The dragging chain was to be discarded and a stout rope substituted. A spare rope with a heavy iron hook, attached to one end, would be prepared, and finally a large strong staple would be fixed firmly into the rear end of the Tar-barrel. Thirty to forty fathoms of stout rope, to say nothing of a heavy hook and staple, cost no small sum, and probably the squad could not have raised a shilling among them. Still, that rope and the hook and the staple were all forthcoming when the Tar-barrel was built. How, will be explained later.

At the appointed hour, the Tar-barrel was set ablaze, and off the squad went down the Garrison Close[6] and on to the Street. Here they were joined by a throng of guizers who, in accordance with custom, added their numbers to the rope, and amid alternate yelling and singing, the Tar-barrel made its way along the Street. By good luck, they reached the Market Cross before the Specials descended on them and annexed the Tar-barrel : the squad faded into the crowd to await the next move by the constables.

[6]Garrison Close:—Charlotte Lane which runs parallel with the south side of Fort Charlotte.

While the usual procedure, on the capture of a Tar-barrel, was to tip it over the banks or into the sea, it occasionally happened that it would be dragged on to an open space, such as the Market Cross, which, at this period, was little better than a beach, and allowed to burn out.   On this occasion the Specials did not have to exert themselves : the Tar-barrel was already on an open space, but to make doubly sure that no attempt would be made to rescue it, the drag-rope was tied round the Market Cross pillar and a guard posted to ensure that no one unmoored it.

While the crowd watched the blazing Tar-barrel, the squad set about preparing for its recapture.   Their plan of action had already been communicated to a number of their friends.   One by one, they aligned themselves ready to receive the spare rope which was passed out to them.   One member of the squad retained the end with the hook and began edging towards the stern of the Tar-barrel and took up a position just behind the inner circle of the spectators.   The leader, concealing a short sharp axe, likewise worked himself into a position near the bow from which he could keep his eyes on the man with the hook.   A signal passed, and simultaneuosly two sack-covered figures burst through the inner ring and dashed towards the Tar-barrel.   Almost at the same time as the hook clanged into the iron staple, the leader brought his axe down on the rope and let out a prodigious yell, "Pull !".

The constables had no time to realise what had happened, and long ere they could take action, the Tar-barrel was careering back through the Street.   To attempt a recapture was out of the question, as it would have been impossible to force a way through the crowd.   The Tar-barrel pursued its course till it reached the north end of the Street and there, amid much cheering and jubilation, it was tipped over the banks below Fort Charlotte, where it fulfilled its destiny as a glorious bonfire.

The next tale concerns a Chief of Police, a worthy man of

the name of Brimms.   Mr Brimms held sway in Lerwick round about the Sixties and was still remembered by several old people up to a few years ago.

It came to Mr Brimms's ears that a squad was burning a Tar-barrel on Hay's Pier, which, at that time, was situated on the site now occupied by the landward end of the Small Boat Harbour breakwater.   This was one of the favourite spots for the final burning, and if a Tar-barrel could run its course and gain the sanctuary of the pier, the police seldom interfered.

On this occasion there must have been a good deal more than the usual hilarity which marked the end of a successful 'run'.   In all probability there was a number of fights in progress, and some of the lieges had deemed it prudent to call in the police, but, whatever the cause, down went Mr Brimms to investigate, and arriving on the scene, he found the disturbers of the peace to be a squad of 'Docks Boys',[7] and the 'Docks Boys' had a well deserved reputation for being a very tough lot.   They resented the Chief's interference, but "when constabulary duty's to be done," Mr Brimms was no shirker, even although subsequent events proved that "his lot was not a happy one".

There was a bit of a fracas, and whether by accident or

design pre-sently Mr Brimms found himself sit-ting in one of the burning tubs.   His exit from the tub was quicker than his entry but,

[7]'Docks Boys':—Lads who lived and worked at Hay's Docks and Garthspool Docks.

even so, his 'latter end' had acquired a liberal supply of burning tar, and with the sleeves of his coat alight, he looked like becoming a veritable fiery cross.

It was a moment for quick decision and Mr Brimms hesitated not.   The edge of the pier was only a yard or two away : Mr Brimms made it in record time and over he went. He was promptly assisted back to 'terra firma,' but history does not relate any sequel—probably none.   It would have been difficult, if not impossible, to identify any of the culprits, or in fact, to collect any evidence at all.

CHAPTER II.

O NE can only conjecture as to how a sledge, loaded with tubs of burning tar, became styled a "Tar-barrel," but it is probable that after the first old tar-barrel was used to augment the bonfire of the festivities, and it was seen how much better the blaze, no bonfire would be complete without one. Gradually the revellers would begin to speak of the bonfire as 'burning the tar-barrel,' and in spite of subsequent changes in the method of burning, the designation 'Tar-barrel' has survived.

In passing, it is of interest to note that the tar-barrel has superseded the bon-fire in other districts than Shetland. There is the annual burning of the 'Clavie' at Burghead on the Moray Firth. Here one half of a tar-barrel, mounted on the end of a stout pole, is used. The barrel is filled with chips and tar, set ablaze and carried over the shoulder of the 'Clavie King' through the streets of the town and thence up to the top of the Doorie Hill where the pole is stuck into a hole in the rock. Then again, in Cornwall there is a custom somewhat analagous to the Shetland 'Tar-barrel' rites.

These survivals of a bye-gone age serve to remind us that the Norse Vikings did not confine their conquests to the Orkney and Shetland Isles, but made their presence felt all round the seaboard of Scotland, down the west coast of England as far as the English Channel, and held Ireland under their sway.

Is it possible then to reconstruct the evolution of the Tar-barrel from its single ancestor till it became the elaborate affair we have under review?

Let us visualise a youth of the single barrel days desiring to add a little more excitement to the proceedings as the folk of his village danced and sang round the blazing bon-fire. Out of sheer devilment, he makes a rush at the barrel and kicks it over, sending it rolling into the circle of revellers who scatter from its path in frantic efforts to avoid the flames and boiling tar. The crowd roars with laughter as first one and then another keeps the barrel careering hither and thither, and it is already certain that this new 'ploy' is marked for repetition at future celebrations.

Youth is ever on the outlook for new ideas : the flaming barrel need no longer be stationary. Why not pull it about and make more fun? One lad would think of placing it on a sledge, and yet another, envious of such ingenuity, would get a brain wave and cut his barrel into halves, and thus outdo his rivals by having two bon-fires. The multiple tub and sledge idea would grow, but with it would arise the necessity of organising a team to make the sledge and afterwards haul it around : the 'squad' system would be evolved.

Competition between squads would follow; more half barrels or tubs would appear on the sledges, but the township roads were narrow and when two squads met, each would challenge the other's right of way. Tempers would break loose and the free fights which followed would be the forerunners of the battles of later days. Whatever its origin, the name 'Tar-barrel' remained, and a few notes on its construction and the methods whereby the necessary materials for its manufacture were obtained, are worth placing on record.

The Tar-barrels of the older 'boys' were known as Four-,

Six-, Eight-, or Ten-tubbers in accordance with the number of tubs used.   The youngsters had smaller replicas, but generally speaking, all were built on the same lines.

The sledge or platform, on which the tubs were placed was known as the 'hatch', no doubt from its similarity to a ship's hatch with which every Shetland lad would be familiar. The length and breadth of the hatch were governed by the number and size of the tubs.   Incidently, the breadth of the Tar-barrel was restricted by the width of the Street, which, in two places, was less than six feet between the buildings on either side.

The sides, which also acted as runners, were made from battens, set parallel on their edges at the requisite distance apart and held securely in position by a platform of stout boards nailed crosswise on top.   At the fore-end was attached a long hauling chain, the end of which was carried back for three or four feet and nailed firmly to each board.

The tubs were made by sawing rum, beer or other casks in half, but if masons' lime tubs could be got, so much the better,

as being saturated and lined with lime, they were more or less fireproof and lasted longer.   The tubs were placed singly or in pairs along the whole length of the hatch and were nailed down very securely.   The reason for this security of nailing will be appreciated later.   Chips and shavings of wood or any other combustible materials were next thrown in and throughly mixed with coal tar.   The Tar-barrel was complete.

No 'jerry building' was permitted in the construction of a Tar-barrel, otherwise it would have been unable to stand the bumps and lurches over the boulders on its journey through Whisky Lane and the steep uneven surface of the Garrison Close before it reached the Street.   Strength, moreover, was of much more importance if, later, it had to try conclusions with another Tar-barrel.   The weight of a Tar-barrel was no mean one : an Eight- or Ten-tubber would weigh anything from twelve hundredweights to a ton.

So far as the youngsters were concerned, it was a case of making anything serve on which they could lay their hands. The bigger boys would try to build their Tar-barrels as nearly as possible to the pattern of their elders.   Anything that would do for a hatch, such as an old gate or door, was used, but when these were not available, it was no uncommon thing for them to dispense with a hatch altogether : a bit of wire, rope or chain was attached to the 'tub' and the tub might be comprised of anything from a bucket, kishie or box to a butter barrel sawn in half.

The actual building of the Tar-barrel was called 'mustering,' and the mustering usually commenced about eight or nine o'clock on the night of the burning and was finished before midnight which was the recognised time for 'lighting-up.'   The youngsters burned their Barrels earlier in the evening.

It was an unwritten but never the less inflexible law that the materials for mustering a tar-barrel must not cost the squad a penny.   Such materials as could not be had for the asking, were 'acquired,' and it was the 'acquiring' which was always considered the most exciting part of the proceedings, but of this more anon.

For weeks before Yule, all the members of a squad would be on the outlook to 'spot' the location of suitable casks or tubs, battens and stout boards of wood. Once these were located, the squad would arrange to meet on a particular night and proceed to remove their 'finds' to places of concealment. Dark, moonless nights were invariably chosen for this purpose and, if the Fates were kind, a nice thick drizzle made them perfect. It was risky to delay removal too long as the legitimate owners might well be on the alert or, worse still, another squad might have ear-marked the same materials. This was no infrequent occurrence, and if another squad were first in 'raiding the roost,' the hunt had to start all over again. Materials had, therefore, to be 'acquired' and hidden a considerable time before the actual night of the mustering.

Long before Lerwick had attained its present dimensions, there stretched, from the foot of what is now Market Street up to where the County Buildings now stand, a rough stony track somewhat resembling the present old Staney Hill road. It was known by the rather suggestive title of Whisky Lane. This track was bounded on each side by the usual dry-stone walls, behind which were grass parks. In the park, bounded by the east wall, were numerous pig-styes with their attendant middens as well as other structures. It has been suggested that this secluded spot was a favourite resort for those who liked to share a bottle in peace and quietness, but whatever the origin of the name, Whisky Lane and the adjoining styes were ideal spots for mustering a Tar-barrel and hiding its constituents away from prying eyes.

Tar was 'acquired' from the Gas Works by the simple expedient of climbing the walls and rolling out a cask of tar or, if the Gas Works manager was so unobliging as not to have one already filled, taking in a barrel and filling it from the tar well.

The squad always knew where they could procure a

dragging chain.   If the one they had used the previous year had been confiscated or lost, well, there were plenty of mooring chains aboard the numerous fishing boats, which were to be had for the taking.   A number of judicious visits to joiner and carpenter shops could be guaranteed to produce an ample supply of large nails and garrons.   Wood chips and shavings could be had for the taking away.

There were three dates on which the Tar-barrels might be burned, namely, 5th, 12th and 29th January, which corresponded with Yule, New Year and Up-Helly-Aa, all old style.   The youngsters were not particular as to which night they burned their Tar-barrels, so long as they could dodge the police, and more especially their parents, who did not look kindly on tarry clothes and burned jackets.

Having decided the date on which they would celebrate, the squad would meet about 8 or 9 p.m. at the spot agreed upon for the mustering.   The first job to undertake was the collection of all the materials from the various 'hidey holes.' This had to be done very circumspectly as it was never known when an inquisitive constable might take it into his head to have a look round, and it would have been a calamity beyond words if, while two of the 'boys' were painfully rolling a barrel of tar across the mud and boulders of Whisky Lane, they suddenly found themselves confronted by a couple of constables who insisted that they had a better right to the tar than the 'boys.'   Whisky Lane and a park just west of the site later occupied by the County Buildings and Prison, were the favourite spots for the mustering.   When visualising these places, the present generation must remember that they were, even then, behind the town and were, in fact, in the country.

As the materials were collected, so would the 'boys' get to work.   Saws and hammers, together with a plentiful supply of nails, would make their appearance, and while some busied themselves with sawing the casks in halves, others would lay out the hatch and cut the platform boards to the proper length. By the dim, fitful light of a candle lantern, the Tar-barrel would gradually take shape till, if all had gone well, it would be ready for its journey before midnight.

While the mustering was going on, it was the duty of one of the junior members to keep watch for prowling policemen, and, at the first signs of alarm, out went the lantern, and silence reigned till the danger was past..

The police, however, do not appear to have made a regular practice of visiting the places where the mustering of a Tar-barrel was going on, but if they did have a look round, it was probably more with a view to reconnaisance than with the idea of making captures. It is related that on one of these infrequent visits, two constables strolled past the spot where a 'muster' was in progress but, although the squad were well aware that they had been discovered, the constables appeared to be quite oblivious to what was going on. It may, of course, have been that discretion was the better part of valour, for they were only two and the squad numbered seven. Later that night, however, a large force of Specials seized the Tar-barrel just as it entered the Street. Yes, on that occasion, discretion was the better part.

CHAPTER III.

A S soon as work on the Tar-barrel was finished, the squad got busy with preparing themselves for their invasion of the town. At this stage of the revelries, members of the squad did not wear their proper guizing dresses : these were only donned after the Tar-barrel had run its course. All other guizers were already in full 'war paint'.

For Tar-barrel rites, there was no uniformity of dress. Some lads preferred a motley collection of old clothes of which a goodly proportion were never designed for masculine wear, but a more general dress was nothing more or less than a sack drawn over the head and body, and from which arm and eyeholes had been cut. This dress, if one could call it such, had the advantage of protecting the wearer, to some extent, from the smoke and heat, but more especially, from the boiling tar which was seldom allowed to remain quietly in the tubs.

The sack-covered guizers presented a truly weird appearance as they worked the Tar-barrel through the Street, and it is little to be wondered at that at least one very small youth thought they were demons from another world. Those of the squad who were dressed in disguises other than sacks, all wore masks of various designs over their heads and faces.

Two of the squad carried long poles, usually oars, with

which they constantly kept stirring up the blazing tubs into yet fiercer flames.   No enviable job this, as, having to keep so close to the Tar-barrel, the heat was terrific, and even with the protection of the sack or mask, many a scorched face was the result.   As the 'Stirrers' worked from one tub to another, the boiling liquid tar, often alight, would fly from the ends of the poles, and woe betide the luckless onlooker who received a scalding blob on face or hands.

The onlookers were not the only people to suffer from the flying tar.   If any of the merchants had had the misfortune to offend the squad, their shop doors and shuttered windows would receive a liberal splashing just by way of intimating to them that they should show a more charitable spirit in future.   It is hardly necessary to add that every ground floor window for the whole length of the Street, was boarded up on Tar-barrel nights.   At about midnight, the Tar-barrel was set alight and started on its journey over the Hillhead, down the Garrison Close and so on to the Street.

A Six- or Eight-tubber was no mean weight and the long drag chain was an unwieldy thing to handle.   The squad by

itself would have made little progress, but from the start, there were always plenty to lend a hand, and when the Street was

reached, there were more than enough guizers only too eager to
get a handgrip on the chain.   Off along the Street they would
go, yelling and cheering, and every now and then, breaking
into marching songs such as "John   Brown's   Body"   and
"Marching Through Georgia".   The words of these songs
were not always the original text, and while those who heard
the singing from a distance were probably thrilled by the martial
music, those who, close at hand, heard the words and the
sentiments thereof, would never have believed that the singers
could ever have attended Sunday school.

Many of the words, although part and parcel of the
ordinary conversation of many of the 'boys,' were of a strength
and vintage which had better be left unrecorded.   There was
no doubt, however, to whom they were applied, and the more
abusive they were to 'Northerner' or 'Southerner'[8] the better.
Crowds of onlookers marched along in front and behind and
all took full part in adding to the din, while here and there,
raucous bellows could be heard above the tumult as some hefty
lads blew and blew again on their looder-horns.[9]

Provided there was no undue interference from the
constables or from other Tar-barrellers, the Tar-barrel would
be dragged from one end of the Street to the other until it began
to show signs of burning out, when it would be halted in some
open space, preferably at the Market Cross or at the Cockstool,[10]
where it would be broken up and made into a bonfire.   By 1 or
1.30 a.m., there would be nothing left but a few glowing
embers, and the squad, having satisfied themselves that these
could be safely left without risk of setting fire to neighbouring
property, would depart to clean up and prepare for guizing :
the night was yet young and the festivities had only just begun.

8'Northerner', 'Southerner':—*See* Chapter 8.

9Looder horn:—A large bullock's horn used by the fishermen of those
days as a fog horn.

10Cockstool:—The name given to a large, humped rock on the beach
just below the Tolbooth.

CHAPTER IV.

SO far, we have followed the Tar-barrel in its smooth uninterrupted passage from the time when the materials were 'acquired' till there remained nothing but a pile of smouldering ashes—now, a grey, dead heap, and then, as the eddying gusts of wind fanned them, springing into glowing life as if longing to live again that fierce joyous hour of homage it had paid to its master, the Sun-god.

But seldom did a Tar-barrel run its course from birth to funeral pyre without incident, and, as a B.B.C. announcer would say, "Here we have Mr Garriock to tell us some of his experiences from his earliest apprenticeship till he became a full-blown Tar-barreller".

"As a small boy, I had gone through the stage of kishie and small box 'tubbers', but these were, of course, more or less back garden affairs, although, no doubt, we felt just as proud of our efforts as any of the older 'boys'. As bigger boys, my chums and I decided that we ought to have a Tar-barrel more like the real thing, but we were not yet at that stage where our pluck had developed sufficiently to risk making raids on the usual places for the coveted materials.

"The squad met as a 'ways and means' committee, and many were the suggestions offered, but as each was considered, it was promptly vetoed by the particular member who was most likely to suffer retribution at the hands of stern parents or irate neighbours.

"It looked as if our ambitious plans were to come to nought when it came into my mind that there was a small spar-red gate at the lower entrance of our garden—the very thing for a hatch, and better still, all ready made.   The other members of the squad, having no cause to fear painful con-sequences, promptly agreed that nothing better could be found : 'find' number one had been located, with the added advantage that it did not require to be hidden.

"The problem of a tub came next ; we were still striving to find a solution when the meeting ended and it was time for us to go home.   Strive as we might, we had simply been unable to think of anything which could have been 'acquired' without too grave a risk of detection.   A night or two later, I was having my weekly hot bath.   It is more than seventy years

since I last saw that tub, but I can still re-member its shining brass hoops and fine metal handles at either end. As I lay enjoying my soak, and more than likely, pondering over the mustering of our Tar-barrel, there came into my mind that the bath would make a very excellent 'tub'.   From idle speculation the idea grew to be a certainty : 'find' number two had been located.

"The collection of the chips and shavings required no planning, as there was an abundance to be had from the carpenters' sheds. The acquisition of an adequate supply of tar presented a more difficult problem. Not one of us knew of anyone in our neighbourhood who had a supply on his premises, and the idea of raiding the Gas Works was, for us youngsters, simply out of the question. It was finally agreed that each boy would, by hook or by crook, try to obtain a tinful. This method of collection was more than justified, as on the appointed day, we had more tar than we required, while one youngster, more daring than his chums, had risked the family wrath by purloining a supply of paraffin which was essential for starting the blaze. The household flask that week, was just a little emptier than usual ; that was all.

"Only one thing more was needed to complete the Tar-barrel : we had no chain. A piece of wire with part of the clothes rope would have done quite well, but now that we were *real* Tar-barrellers, nothing less than a real chain would do. An intensive search among the small rowing boats, drawn up on the beach at Twagios, resulted in our spotting the very thing we required, and on the night before our 'burning,' it was removed and hidden.

"On Christmas night we mustered our One-tubber, and, dressed as nearly as we could after the fashion of our elders, no prouder squad ever dragged out its blazing masterpiece till it had gone the way of all good Tar-barrels. The following night we quietly returned the chain to the boat from which it had been borrowed, but when next my weekly bath became due, the bath tub could not be found and its disappearance remained an unsolved mystery.

"As we grew older it was only natural that we should, more and more, desire to emulate the ways of our seniors in the art of 'acquiring' the wherewithal for the mustering of our Tar-barrels. We were apt pupils and we quickly learned not to 'axe'[11] for what we wanted : we just went and took it.

"Our ambitions too were growing with the years and we had reached the stage when One-tubbers were much too juvenile. Nothing less than a Three-tubber would now satisfy us and we set about looking for the necessary materials for its construction. I have forgotten from where we got the battens and boards for the hatch, but more than likely from some builder's yard. The tubs came from three kind-hearted housewives who, most conveniently for us, were in the habit of leaving them outside their back doors at night. The tubs just disappeared.

"We next turned our attention to the Gas Works, which were unobtrusively surveyed daily until it was noted there were some handy casks of tar available. On a pitch-black night, we met outside the Gas Works, and after making sure that there was no one about, we scaled the walls and dropped down safely on the other side. It was certainly dark outside the walls, but inside, in the shadow of the gasometer and the buildings, the darkness was of an intensity which could be felt.

"Now, we knew exactly where the casks lay, but it was surprising how elusive they became. We found, or rather our shins did, many things which were not casks and one boy carried away a souvenir of our visit in the shape of a badly bruised forehead which had come in contact with one of the gasometer weights. I was just beginning to wonder whether the whole outlay of the Gas Works had been altered within the past twentyfour hours, when I heard a low but jubilant voice exclaiming 'A'm fun' dem'.

"The handiest cask seemed to be nearly full of tar but it had no bung. No raiding squad ever entered the Gas Works without providing for such an emergency and we, too, had our

---

[11] 'Axe':—The motto on all Up-Helly-Aa Bills is "We axe for what we want". A sketch of a battle axe accompanies the motto. 'Axe' is Shetlandic for 'ask'.

bung—a round tapered plug of wood designed to fit any ordinary cask bunghole. We lost no time in driving in the bung and started to roll out the cask. The double gates were, of course, locked, with one half held in position by means of a hooked bar attached to the gate pillar. We simply unhooked the bar and disengaged the lock by drawing both halves inwards. The gates were open and, rolling out our prize, we set off.

"We were, however, very unlucky in our choice of cask as, before proceeding many yards, we found it covered with liquid tar. An examination revealed that the bunghole was a square one. Square bungholes were not uncommon and an older squad would not have been caught napping, but we were young and this was our first foray. Speak of laying a trail ! We were doing it with a vengeance. Something had to be done and that quickly. There was no time to get a square bung so the next best thing was to try to make the round one serve. Handkerchiefs were requisitiond and rolled round the bung which was again jammed in as best we could.

"Off we went again, trundling the cask along the Docks Road (Commercial Road), up Whisky Lane and so on to the pig-styes at the back of Fort Charlotte where the Territorial Drill Hall and adjacent buildings now stand. The handkerchiefs had only partially stopped the leak, and most of the lining of my coat had gone to supplement them. What a mess we were in, but the styes were reached at last and, digging a hole in one of the middens, in went the cask with the bunghole uppermost and the midden was restored to its former appearance.

"Reaching home and letting myself in through my bedroom window, I spent most of the rest of the night cleaning up and trying, most unsuccessfully, to remove the tar from my clothes. Fortunately for me they were old ones and I escaped being asked awkward questions.

"We fixed on Christmas for the date of our 'burning,'

and to complete the illusion that we were now really 'big' guizers, we mustered our Tar-barrel in one of the approved spots in a park behind the present site of the County Buildings. We were of course, 'big' guizers, but when it came to invading the Street, our courage failed us, and our Tar-barrel was burned on the Hillhead where there was little or no risk of interference.

"The days of my apprenticeship were now nearly over and it was a very proud day for me when a chum and I were asked to join an older ' boys' ' squad. This did not mean that we were now full-blown Tar-barrellers, and although we were admitted to the councils of the squad, we were very soon made to understand that our job was to listen and do what we were told. In fact, for the first year our duties were more in the nature of acting as fags and scouts to our elders. Still, we were members of a 'big' squad and that was all that mattered.

"At our first meeting—a proud day that—we were told that the squad had decided to have a Six-tubber, and we received orders to scout round and try to locate where tubs and barrels for tar might be found. Next day, two lads might have been seen quietly strolling here and there about the premises at the Docks. To all appearance they were just two of many other youngsters who played around the boats drawn up on the foreshore or clambered over piles of wood, but their eyes were everywhere and windows in various stores seemed to have a peculiar fascination for them. After a time they wandered away home and that night reported the results of their scouting to the squad.

"Choosing a suitable night, the squad met about midnight : three members were allocated the task of collecting the tubs which had been spotted through a window in one of the curing sheds. To us was assigned the role of guides. The two remaining members were deputed to secure the barrels for the tar. These were lying in an open shed in another yard and their removal was accomplished without encountering any difficulty.

"Our party, having arrived at the shed where the tubs were stored, found the door secured by a padlock fastened to a hasp and staple. To draw the staple quietly was the work of seconds, and opening the door we proceeded to remove the tubs.

"Now, it so happened that these particular premises were ones which had suffered frequently in the past from raids by the Tar-barrellers, and as the tar-barrelling season was approaching, the foreman was on the alert and carrying out nightly rounds. The first intimation we had of his presence was the sound of a gruff voice at the door shouting, 'What the hell are you doing there?' 'What the hell is that your business?' came the reply from one of the tougher 'boys'. The foreman did not stop to argue the point but made a rush at the intruders : a stave descended 'whack' on his pate and he took no further interest in the proceedings.

"Needless to say, I was shocked and more than a little scared at my introduction to the ways of the older 'boys', but for the good name of all genuine old Tar-barrellers, I am glad to be able to say that this was the only occasion of which there is any record of such callous behaviour. Fight ! Yes, they would fight, but fight square and above board. That incident took place more than sixty years ago, but even to this day, I shudder to think what might have been the result of that cowardly attack. At the time, however, I dared not show any feelings in the matter, and we went off carrying our spoils. A little later we were joined by the other two members with the barrels, and everything was successfully hidden.

"A night or two later, the barrels were taken to the Gas Works where they were filled from the tar-well while we two youngsters kept watch. After being filled, the barrels were rolled across the road and hidden below the banks just north of where Groat's Bakery now stands.

"At that time, the ground to the north of the Gas Pier was an open beach with a path across it leading to the Northness curing stations. The beach was mainly used as a wintering stance for rowing boats of which there was then a great number in Lerwick. The boats were drawn up close under the banks, and it was between the boats and the banks, and partly into the bank itself that we dug a hole into which we put the barrels. The hole was filled up and a boat drawn well over it to hide the signs of excavation. By the time we had finished, we were more than satisfied that our tar was safe till we wanted it.

" 'The best laid schemes o' mice and men gang aft agley' : two days later we were told that the barrels had been unearthed and removed by the police. This was indeed a blow which looked like wrecking all our plans. We had decided to burn the Tar-barrel on Yule morning and Yule was now only three days off. Well we knew that no opportunity would be given us to raid the Gas Works again during the next two nights, and without tar there could be no Tar-barrel.

"Luck, however, did not desert us; by dint of persistent enquiry, we heard of a squad who had planned their 'burning' for Up-Helly-Aa, and elicited the information that they had already made their raid and had a full supply of tar safely hidden away. To them our leaders went and, after a good deal of persuasion and making solemn promises that we would replace all tar borrowed, they agreed to let us have what we required. On Yule morning we burned our Six-tubber, and about ten nights later we once again visited the Gas Works and implemented our promises.

"The loss of our tar had a sequel. The late John

Robertson of the Trance,[12] incidentally, my uncle, was in the habit of taking a walk every morning out to his curing station at Northness.   As luck would have it, on the very morning on which our barrels were removed, he was seen in conversation with the Chief Constable.   The 'boys' put two and two together, and Mr Robertson, rightly or wrongly, was blamed for giving away the whereabouts of the hiding place.

"Such a breach of 'good manners' could not be tolerated and Mr Robertson would have to be taught a lesson.   Early on Christmas Eve, the squad hastily mustered a small Four-tubber and brought it to the Street.   Passing Mr Robertson's shop, it was halted and kept standing there long enough to blister all the paint off the door and window.   In fact, the door had actually caught fire before the Tar-barrel was removed, and Mr Robertson had to face the expense of repainting and graining.   The reason for this retribution was only revealed to me after the deed had been done but I am quite certain that, even had I known beforehand what the squad had planned, I should not have dared to give my uncle warning.

"I could go on relating tales of the squad, but they would be, more or less, similar to those already told except that never again, in our raids for materials, did we encounter another over-zealous custodian of things we wished to 'acquire'.

"To our squad, however, fell the honour of mustering the largest Tar-barrel that was ever dragged through the Street and finally burned as a bon-fire above the Cockstool.   Not only was it the largest but it was the last to run a successful course before Tar-barrelling was absolutely prohibited.   (Three further attempts were made—two in 1876 and one in 1878— but all three were frustrated by the police.)   It was a Twelve-

---

[12]The Trance :—Mr Robertson's shop, 66 Commercial Street, got its name from the fact that at one time this part of Commercial Street was bridged over between his shop and the building on the opposite side of the street. At least one old map of Lerwick shows two other trances over Commercial Street.

tubber measuring twenty-four feet in length and just over five feet in width, and it is of interest to record that all the timber used in its construction was purloined from the adjacent County Buildings which were then in course of erection.

"The intention had been to muster a Ten-tubber, and the requisite number of tubs had already been secured. The battens, however, proved to be twenty-four feet in length, and, while we were removing these, we accidentally stumbled on some masons' lime tubs, two of which we took along with us. No squad had ever before attempted to muster a Twelve-tubber, but now we had all the materials with which to make one. More than one of the squad expressed doubts as to its being a practical proposition, but the incentive to create a new record soon outweighed all objections, and a Twelve-tubber was mustered.

"The objectors were right : it proved to be a most unwieldy affair, and I doubt if ever again would such a large one have been attempted, even had Tar-barrelling been allowed to go on. There were plenty of guizers available to man its great drag chain but it was difficult to manoeuvre in the tortuous, narrow, winding street. It was only possible to negotiate the corners by making use of a trip rope and levers—no enviable job this, as the stern-crew had, all the time, to work in the smoke and heat coming from the tubs. This Tar-barrel, like its predecessors, was mustered in the afore-mentioned park near the site of the County Buildings, and the last obsequies were carried out at the Cockstool on Yule morning, 5th January, 1874. Before another Yule had come around, the authorities had definitely and finally banned the Tar-barrel.

"Never again will one small youngster be heard saying to another 'Düs du ken dat dir musterin' a Tar-barrel up i' da Whisky Lane? I wiss midder wid lat me bide oot an' see hit, bit shö says a'm to geng ta me bed an' no be a gaapis (fool). May-be I wul : Is du comin'? We could aisy rin

up da Gerrison Closs and be doon in nae time, an' hae a
peerie (little) keek ower da waa. Midder wid never ken' ''.

"That small youngster recalls to me two tricks we used
to play on the police when, as small boys, we anticipated,
or it would be nearer the truth to say, deliberately planned,
that our Tar-barrel should fall into the hands of the police.

"I have mentioned that the small boys' Tar-barrel was
usually a box or a kishie and that a piece of wire with a rope
attached served as a substitute for a chain. When we were
out to trick the police, the wire was dispensed with, and, if
we were in luck, a policeman would be after us before the
rope had burned through. As soon as we saw him, one of the
boys would cut the rope and off we would skedaddle. From
a safe distance in the crowd—there was always a crowd—we
would watch the constable trying to remove the fiery furnace
but the unequal contest usually ended with it being allowed
to burn out where it stood.

"The second trick was just a variation of the first. A
staple was fixed to the fore-end of the hatch, and through it
was passed the chain or rope, the loose ends being held together
as we marched along. At the first cry of 'Police !', one
end was dropped and the chain run off as we made our feet
our friend. These tricks could not be done with the heavy
Tar-barrels of the older 'boys' but to us younger fry they
were a perfect delight''.

CHAPTER V.

IT has already been mentioned that the authorities frowned on the practice of Tar-barrelling, and that they had good cause for the attitude they took up, there can be little doubt. The Editor of the *Shetland Times* of the 'Seventies had a particular antipathy to Tar-barrelling, and, in all the early issues of this paper, he either condemns the practice outright or, after it was banned, rejoices greatly at its termination. On 11th January, 1874, he writes, "Of course there was a tar-barrel drawn through Commercial Street but, except for leaving the public thoroughfare in not a pleasant condition for pedestrians, no other damage was done".

On 11th January, 1875, after Tar-barrelling had been banned, he commences his report on the festivities thus : "Christmas Day (Old Style)—Christmas day was held here on Tuesday last, and, so far as we can learn, passed off very quietly. Although there was boisterous mirth in the guizing line, there were no unseemly attempts made at dragging tar-barrels through the town, as in previous years, to the annoyance and damage to the lieges. On this occasion our young people acted wisely, going in with the wishes of their more quiet and sedate neighbours. We trust we have witnessed the last of the tar-barrel nuisance : there was neither pleasure nor profit in it—nothing but soiled clothes and besmeared skins. We, therefore, congratulate our young folk on the pleasant Christmas spent, and hope—for their sake—that we may have as pleasing a duty to perform in chronicling the New Year (old style) rejoicings".

The Editor's wish was gratified, and his 'chronicles', on 18th January, are well worth recording almost in full. This is what he says : "Since the entrance of Seventy-Five upon its eventful course, we have had our accustomed festivities; and, when asked to express our convictions regarding their form, we have not hesitated to acknowledge a very considerable improvement on the past. Instead of the time-honoured tar-barrel with its hurdle and chains, its noxious smoke and scorching flame, its yelling imps and barbarous dances, its masquerade and saturnalia, inspiring fear and threatening destruction of property and life, we have had a season of repose and rational enjoyment. Even the cases of glass breaking have fallen from the hundred to two, and the wanton mischief of many has given place to restrained mirth. . . . Instead, therefore, of requiring to chronicle a number of hair-breadth escapes and bodily fractures, broken panes and burned doors, marred houses and tar stained streets, we have the more pleasant task to perform and we hail with satisfaction the alteration which Magisterial wisdom and firmness have inaugurated. . . . The general public feel satisfied that we have entered upon a new era of rational and reputable Christmas and New Year practices".

In the following year, 1876, on 8th January, the Editor continues his pæans of praise over the disappearance of the Tar-barrel, but one sentence culled from them will suffice : "The nuisance of tar-barrels seems now—at least we hope so—to be fairly abolished, and to be reckoned among the barbarisms of a bye-gone age." That phrase "at least we hope so" indicates that the Editor is not altogether sure that "Magisterial wisdom and firmness" will be effective. That he had reason for his qualifying phrase, is evidenced by the following letter to the *Times* from "A Citizen" on 29th January of the same year :—

"Sir,—Last night our community was again disgraced and our streets destroyed by the exertions of a few low black-guards, and, though it is said that some have been identified, those silly blockheads have most likely been the dupes of the real perpetrators who—coward like—meanly kept themselves from the consequences. It is to be hoped that both parties will be delighted with their dirty work".

This letter inspired "A Lerwick Boy" to reply in the following issue of the paper, thus :—

"Sir,—When I read the letter from 'A Citizen' in your last paper, I says to myself that he is some new-come fellow for no real Lerwick boy will believe that we are blackguards for having a tar-barrel and none of our old companions will credit that we are cowardly—they know better than that. The stupid fellows who allowed themselves to be known have themselves to thank. Had they obeyed orders, held their tongues, and kept their masques properly on, there would have been no danger, as the constables were afraid to touch us. If these fellows had been real Lerwick boys, they would have had more sense, and we are going to pay for them if they are fined, and also to pay William Mouat for the tar, because he is a poor man, and we could not get the tar any other way. Sir, you will excuse me signing my name, but I just wanted every Lerwick boy to know that we are still honour bright".

In allowing this anonymous letter to be published, the Editor comments : "To oblige 'A Lerwick Boy' we departed from our usual custom, and have inserted his letter without knowing who the writer is. We assure the writer that we most heartily sympathise with the boys of the town on all that is noble and of great repute, and we are very glad to learn that they intend to act 'honour bright' in this matter. But, we venture to ask, do our young friends think the game is worth the candle? We have heard stories of heroism of 'Lerwick Boys' that have made our hearts beat and the tear come to our eyes but such stories were never in connection with a tar-barrel''.

Two weeks later, on 19th February, the *Times* reports the sequel : "Three men were brought up at the Court on Wednesday, charged with taking part in the dragging of a burning tar-barrel through the town on the evening of 28th ult. All three pleaded not guilty, but, after proof, the Sheriff found the charge proven against two, and sentenced them to eight days' imprisonment each. We are sorry to say the two found guilty were married men''.

These extracts from the *Shetland Times* throw a very vivid light on the 'ongoings' of the Tar-barrellers as viewed by the authorities and the more law-abiding citizens of old Lerwick. The art, or rather the sensationalism, of present day reporting was not in vogue in those days, so we get no description of a Tar-barrel with its weirdly dressed crew, its progress through the town, its clashes with the police or even of the 'battles royal' between rival squads. With such events taking place to-day, Lerwick would be invaded with a host of special reporters, equipped with 'movie' cameras and magnesium flares, to 'cover' the 'Survival of Fireworship in the Far North'. The Editor of the *Shetland Times* simply records, "Of course there was a tar-barrel drawn through Commercial Street''.

CHAPTER VI.

THE case for the Prosecution has been set out in no uncertain
manner, but our Counsel for the Defence pleads an
emphatic "Not Guilty". He will not even admit
'extenuating circumstances' : in fact, he maintains that the
police have arraigned the wrong parties altogether. He frankly
admits one most regrettable lapse—the cowardly attack on the
foreman—but avers that that was the exception which proved
the rule. Let us, therefore, hear what he has to say.

"I admit that the authorities frowned on the Tar-barrel,
but even so, a great deal of latitude was given and, generally
it would be allowed to run its course, provided the guizers kept
their spirits within bounds. Towards the end of the Tar-
barrelling days, however, a great deal of malicious mischief
was done, and this was, most unwarrantably, laid on the
shoulders of the Tar-barrellers. I was a fervent Tar-barreller
from early youth up to the time when Tar-barrelling was
finally prohibited, and I can truthfully say that I never knew a
single Tar-barreller who purposely set out to do malicious
damage.

"What's that?" exclaims the reader. "Do you call
bare-faced theft and assault with violence within the law?
You do have a queer idea of right and wrong : within the

law indeed! What about these tarred windows and burned doors?" "The assault I admit, but it was an isolated instance and one which I heartily condemned. Besides 'one swallow does not make a summer' nor does one regrettable incident condemn a time-honoured institution.

" 'Tarring' was the recognised method of bringing home to curmudgeons that 'spoil sports' and miserable spirits would not be tolerated during the festive season; not a legal method but one which met with the singular approval of all healthy minded citizens. Is there a single one among you who could not name some person you know who would be none the worse of being taught a lesson in tolerance and whom you would not cheerfully put in the pillory? Our way was 'Tar Law'—reprehensible, illegal, call it what you will, it was effective.

"Further, from generation to generation, Tar-barrelling had been part and parcel of the Yule festivities, and, even if the despoiled of to-day had not been, themselves, the despoilers of yesterday, they would in all probability have taken part in Tar-barrel fun in their youth. There could have been very few men in Lerwick who had not, in their youth, gone out guizing, and I never yet met a guizer who was not only too eager to join up with the others when a Tar-barrel made its appearance. They knew everything there was to know about the game, and their general attitude was that if you could 'pinch' and get away with it, 'Well, it is just what we used to do ourselves'.

"And there they were content to leave matters, but, when gates in front of houses were removed, pillars torn down, dwelling house windows tarred and the street gas lamps smashed, the patience of the most enthusiastic old Barrellers got exhausted and Tar-barrelling was put under sentence of death. In every community there are youths whose sole idea of amusement is perpetrating malicious mischief, and the nights of Tar-barrelling and Guizing were the very ones on which they could smash and destroy with impunity under the shelter of the revelry which was going on elsewhere.

"No genuine Tar-barreller could have found time for such mischief : each one was hard at work from early evening until the 'burning' was over. After that they had to clean up and get ready for the house-to-house guizing proper, and, as the guizing went on for the remainder of the night till break-fast-time next morning, they had no chance or inclination for other ploys. Finally, if we made such a mess of people's houses with tarry feet, is it not very remarkable that the same people opened their houses and welcomed us to them year after year?"

The obvious title for the next chapter ought to be "The Summing Up and The Verdict", but no matter how well the judge might sum up, a jury of high-spirited youth and sedate old age would certainly disagree. Let us leave it at that.

CHAPTER VII.

THE AFTERMATH.

THE authorities had definitely prohibited Tar-barrelling in 1874, but three further attempts were made to revive it. One, already noted, was made on Up-Helly-Aa, 1876, when two of the squad were caught and imprisoned. According to the evidence of those who remember this revival, it was poorly planned and deserved its fate. In this year, also, another attempt was foiled by the police.

Old customs die hard, and two years later a better planned and much more determined effort was made. A squad of 'old timers' determined to live once again the few thrilling hours which had been their birth-right in years gone by. They 'acquired' the materials in the orthodox way; they hid them in the same old places of concealment in the styes and huts adjoining Whisky Lane, and they mustered their Tar-barrel on Up-Helly-Aa, 1878.

Somehow or other the news leaked out and the Specials were out in force. A strong squad was posted at the foot of the Garrison Close, the usual place of entry to the Street, and yet another posse patrolled the south end. The squad was kept informed of the dispositions of the police forces and made their plans accordingly.

At the appointed hour of midnight, they set their Barrel

ablaze, and with plenty willing helpers they dragged it over the Hillhead, and rushed it down Swallow Lane (Union Bank Lane) and on to the Street. Such was the speed with which they carried out this manoeuvre that they almost reached the Market Cross before the converging squads of Specials hemmed them in and seized the Tar-barrel. It was hauled on to the Cross and there the 'last of the line' departed in a blaze of glory. No arrests were made.

Mention has been made of the wanton destruction of property by youths who had no connection with the Tar-barrellers. The prohibition of the custom, however, did not, as it was hoped, put an end to outbursts of malicious damage and rowdyism. So far as records are available, nothing serious occurred during the Yule festivities of 1875, and the Editor of the *Shetland Times* congratulates everyone on having "entered a new era," but the new era was of short duration.

In 1876 he bemoans the attempted revival of the Tar-barrel, but of Up-Helly-Aa, 1877, he is moved to report that "in fact it might almost be called a revival of the old festival, and several incidents in connection with it we would have gladly reported, only it was accompanied with such an amount of malicious mischief, in the way of breaking doors and windows, that we are ashamed to make it known to our friends abroad".

This Editorial criticism brought forth from a correspondent a letter of about one thousand words. For the most part it is written in a facetious style, and in lurid terms describes the wholesale destruction of the town. It then proceeds to make sly hits at various elders who are said to have been celebrating —"one with his hat on the back of his head; another was observed to walk along with uncertain steps and with a huge bottle in his pocket bearing the legend 'Lemonade'. Another was scanning the starry sky with a gigantic telescope which on nearer approach resolved itself into a bottle." Yet another "was seen throwing little stones into the sea but it was re-marked that he put away every other stone into his pocket".

We were puzzled by this reference to the elder who amused himself by pocketing pebbles from the beach, especially as more than one elder was said to have acquired a supply. Later on, one gathers from the context that these 'pillars of the kirk' were laying in a store of ammunition which was to to be used in smashing the street lamps. The letter continues : "All we ask is that they should confess their error and pay Parlie for the lamps". 'Parlie' was the nickname of the then lamp-lighter whose contract apparently included the upkeep as well as the lighting of the street lamps.

The elders having been duly castigated, the writer suggests that members of the Town Council were not wholly innocent of having a share in the lawlessness of Up-Helly-Aa. "Can they all lay their hand upon their thigh and swear that they were not out on Up-Helly-Aa? . . . Rumour, however, with her hundred tongues hath not been silent" and so on, but the Councillors, in contrast with the elders, seem to have been a sober lot.

The writer signs himself "The 6, 9 or 12 (as the case may be) Clerical Missionaries". Apparently, as Clerical Missionaries, their attempts at the conversion of the community on Up-Helly-Aa do not appear to have been very successful, in spite of the very clever Appeal which they distributed. (See Appendix IV).

A close study of the criticisms of the Times of the previous week and the contents of this letter, makes one wonder whether there was not a certain amount of collusion between the Editor and the writer of the letter with a view to revealing the 'certain incidents' which he hesitated to report.

That the rowdyism and mischief of Up-Helly-Aa, 1877, were worse than usual, is borne out by the fact that the Town Council and Commissioners of Police met under the chairmanship of Major Cameron, senior bailie, to consider 'the breaking of windows and street lamps on 29th January last' and to hear a 'letter from Mr Galloway, Procurator Fiscal, and the reply the Magistrates had instructed him (the Clerk) to write in answer'.

In his letter Mr Galloway stated "that the attention of the Sheriff has been called to the proceedings on the night of Monday, 29th January, and he wishes to know what the Magistrates propose to do. The Sheriff suggests that 'it might also be a very salutary thing' if they evoked section 85 of the Lindsay Act to impose a Special Riots Assessment and from it, not only claims of damages but also the expense of preventative measures, such as additional constables, say from 25th December to 1st February might be defrayed. Something must be done, and the Sheriff will be glad to know what the Magistrates propose to do".

The Magistrates instructed the Town Clerk to reply "that the Magistrates and Town Council have been doing what they could, and are still doing what they can, to trace the persons who were guilty of breaking windows on the night of 29th January last, but from the fact that so many who were out that evening were disguised, evidence has not been obtained, though certain persons are suspected to have had connection with the damage done. In the hope that the efforts which are being made otherwise to detect the parties, may be intensified, a reward of £10 shall be offered to any person adducing evidence which will lead to a conviction. On the night in question there were on beat in the Burgh three special constables, well selected men, besides the Superintendent of Police. The Magistrates desire me further to say that they will bring before the Commissioner of Police, on an early opportunity, the suggestion made as to the imposition of a Special Riots Assessment".

The next issue of the *Shetland Times* contains the

following announcement :—''The Magistrates and Town Council have offered a reward of £10 for any evidence that may lead to the conviction of the parties concerned in breaking the windows and street lamps on the night of 29th January last''.

It is apparent from the Clerk's reply to Mr Galloway that there were only three special constables on duty on the night of Up-Helly-Aa, and it would, therefore, seem that the Authorities, in view of the prohibition of Tar-barrelling and the orderliness of the festivities in the previous year, did not consider a large force necessary.

There is no record that the offer of the £10 reward led to the conviction of anyone concerned in the breaking of windows and street lamps. That the Town Council, however, had taken to heart the advice of the Sheriff, is evidenced by a ''NOTICE'' in the *Shetland Times* of 17th November, 1877, in which ''the Town Council, acting as Commissioners have . . . . LAID ON and IMPOSED the POLICE ASSESSMENT . . . . an Assessment of twopence in the pound . . . . to defray certain charges and expenses incurred by the Local Authority . . . . ''.

A much larger number of special constables was enrolled for duty during the ensuing festive season, and the determination of the Authorities to put a stop to riotous behaviour, had a quietening effect on the law-breakers. No more incidents are recorded until January, 1883, when ''sundry small acts of mischief along the street'' occurred which brought forth the Editorial comment that ''the whole affair appeared to be an organised attempt in the interest of those who make a great parade of keeping up 'old institutions' ''.

On Christmas, 1884, there was more trouble, but the Editor, perhaps in deference to the feelings of 'our friends abroad', simply comments that there was ''much shouting, Bacchanalian songs and other seasonable noises''. One could scarcely call this a serious indictment, but there must have been a good deal more hooliganism and rowdyism than is implied by the foregoing description, as, later in the report, we are informed that "the special constables came out, marshalled by the zealous Superintendent of Police, and were stationed at points of vantage . . . . Each was armed to the teeth with a nine-inch club, this weapon being specially constructed for the purpose . . . . After the arrival of these guardians of the peace, order was restored".

The tide of malicious mischief was rising again, and a great amount of damage to windows, gas lamps and doors was done on New Year's morning and on Up-Helly-Aa. The Editor is now not so sure about the efficacy of the special constables : "It certainly seems strange that such mischief could have been wrought while constables were stationed along the street and roads; but, whether the perpetrators be brought to justice or not, there is no doubt that they, by their conduct, have put the pastime, in which they were doubtless engaged, in danger of forever being forbidden by the authorities".

The police, however, did manage to arrest one young man who was brought before Bailie Robertson, and charged with breaking a street lamp. The report of this case takes up four columns of the *Times*, but, although it makes lively reading, it is much too long to quote in full. Mr J. B. Anderson, solicitor, appeared for the defence, and the Court was packed to overflowing. Proof was led, and the accused was found guilty : he was fined one and a half guineas with the option of twenty days' imprisonment. The report concludes :—"The sentence was received with most unwonted expression of feeling, a perfect storm of hisses and hooting mingled with roars of laughter ensuing, and, while the tumult lasted, which it did for several moments, nothing could be heard but a confused babel of voices. Bailie Robertson endeavoured to restore order but his voice was utterly lost amid the general uproar".

Following the disposal of this case, another young man was brought forward and charged with attempting to rescue "a prisoner whom the constables had in custody", the prisoner being the previous accused. He, also, was convicted on proof and fined 10/6 with the option of eight days' imprisonment.

To have entitled this chapter "The Aftermath" is, perhaps, not strictly correct. Although, after the ban on Tar-barrelling, three attempts were made to revive the custom, the malicious damage recorded can hardly be attributed to disgruntled Barrellers. It has been shewn that a great deal of malicious mischief did take place in Tar-barrelling days and was probably the principal reason for its prohibition. Nevertheless, the wilder elements among the youth of the town, being deprived of the fun and excitement of the Tar-barrels, may have been influenced in a greater degree to increase their desires to commit wanton mischief.

CHAPTER VIII.

THE TALE OF A CANNON.

TO the Lerwegian of today, Fort Charlotte is just a bit
of old Lerwick which has been built-in all around by
roads, dwelling houses, shops and stores. He passes along
a broad highway below the Fort, or takes a short-cut through
it, but seldom does he trouble to give the old place a single
thought.

Eighty years ago, its presence would have been forced
upon him, whether he liked it or not, for the Fort was not
then 'just a bit of old Lerwick'. It still dominated the town
and harbour over which it seemed to keep a watchful eye.

Seen from the sea, it presented a stern, solid frontage of
rock around whose base ran a narrow, winding road and a
beach. No building obscured its view from the north, west,
east or southeast, and its old guns looked out through the

ramparts as if giving challenge to all who would dare to do hurt to the town over whose destinies it had stood guard for more than two centuries.

On a fine, bright winter day just before Yule, 1860,[13] there might have been seen a band of youths, sitting on the remains of an old rowing boat, deeply engaged in earnest conversation. What they were discussing is not recorded, but if one were asked to guess, it would probably be very near the mark, to answer that they were making up the 'ploys' they would be 'after doing' during the coming Yule festivities.

As the conversation rambled on, one youth allowed his eyes to rest on the black muzzle of one of the guns on the ramparts above. There was nothing new in the appearance of the guns to hold his attention : he had gazed upon them hundred of times before, but that day they seemed to have a peculiar fascination for him. His brows were knit in meditation and his eyes had a far-away look. One of his chums addressed a remark to him, but he did not seem to hear it, or, if he did, he certainly did not comprehend its purport, as the only answer he made was "Yea, I dü believe hit cud be dön". This cryptic remark called for elucidation, and, by the time its meaning had been made plain, the excited gestures and exclamations of the 'boys' and their frequent upward glances at the guns, showed that the thing which he 'believed cud be dön' had met with their enthusiastic approval.

Whether or not they had been discussing 'ploys' before, they were now planning one which would go down in history as one of the most daring that had ever been attempted. In previous years they had made and fired many a cracker and bomb, but these were to be mere child's play compared with what they were now scheming to do. It was nothing other

---

[13]1860 :—Efforts have been made, without success, to establish the year but, among the dwindling number of those who knew the details of the incident recorded, the general opinion is that it took place on New Year's morning, 1861.

than to bring in the New Year by loading and firing one of the cannon. That they were proposing to commit a felony did not in the least alarm them, and it is quite certain that, even had they given this aspect of the matter a thought, their decision would have been the same : their only worry was how to carry out their project without being caught.

To the reader, such a 'ploy' has the appearance of impossibility, if not of sheer madness, for how could any one person, much less a band of youths, enter one of Her Britannic Majesty's fortresses, load and fire a cannon without being caught? Impossible ! It was, however, not really so difficult as it would appear. At that time there was, more or less, free ingress and egress to and from the Fort. It had long ceased to be used as a place of defence ; the barracks no longer housed the red-coats, and such uniforms as were still to be seen, were those of the Navy. The War Office had, many years before, leased it to the Admiralty, who now used it as a Coast Guard and Training Station.

The naval personnel lived within the walls of the Fort, but some of the dwelling houses were let to private citizens, and the court house and prison were in the building which is now occupied by the Y.M.C.A. Red Triangle Club. There was always a watchman on duty, but, even after dark, persons coming and going through the gate-ways aroused little interest and less comment.

The squad had very little difficulty in obtaining an ample supply of gunpowder, but, in what manner, had better not be enquired into too closely, as, in accordance with custom, costs did not enter into the scheme of things so far as Tar-barrelling and ploys were concerned. The powder was sewn up into bags in the regular navy style, and a small quantity was reserved for the priming.

Up till now, the 'boys' had had only one thought, and

that was the bang which would follow the firing of the gun, but now someone suggested that it would be a pity to waste all that good powder without having some shot. The rest of the squad agreed but, on the whole, they did retain some sense, as none of the so-called 'shot' was solid or hard enough to do much material damage should it find a target. Asked long afterwards, what they had actually used as shot, one of the 'boys' replied "'O' jist a lok o' muck" which he said included a cabbage, an old boot, peats and anything that could be carried conveniently, not forgetting the gamey remains of a dead cat, though this latter was an afterthought.

The time for carrying out the ploy was fixed for midnight on New Year's Eve, and, on that night, had the naval contingent in the Fort elected to stop and search all intruders, they would have collected a dossier of information which would have startled and puzzled My Lords at Whitehall. Bags of gunpowder, concealed under the jackets of several men entering Government property, would have conjured up visions of another Gunpowder Plot; the bearer of the cabbage might have pled that it was part of the household provender, and even the lad with the old boot might have concocted a tale, however unconvincing, about his taking it home for repair; but it is difficult to imagine any story which would have explained away the remains of poor Tabby.

It would have been interesting to speculate on what My Lords would have said or done, but this would be idle, because no startling arrests were made. It was between 11 p.m. and midnight on New Year's Eve that several inconspicuous figures might have been seen casually passing through the gates of the Fort. They were all carrying parcels, but on New Year's Eve, almost more than on any other night, such a thing would give no cause for suspicion.

Once inside the Fort, they quietly crawled up the grassy

embankment below the ramparts and assembled by the most southerly gun which, of all the cannon, was furthest away from curious eyes. With an improvised ramrod, the bags of gunpowder were rammed home, and this was followed by the assorted 'lok o' muck' with pussy as the final plug. The priming was run into the touch-hole and the match laid. All being prepared for the final act, the squad quietly dispersed, leaving one of their number crouching beside the cannon.

Slowly the minutes passed, but at last the clock on the old Tolbooth tower struck the midnight hour : the crouching figure straightened himself, bent over the gun, and shielding his flint and steel with his cap, he ignited the match. Then he, too, quietly disappeared. Except for a tiny red spark slowly spluttering towards the touch-hole, all was quiet once more on the ramparts.

Not for long did this peace remain. Suddenly the stillness of the night was shattered by a terrific bang which shook the houses in the vicinity like an earthquake. Guizers on the Street thought the powder magazine had blown up. Terrified citizens rushed to their doors as the glass from their blown-in windows clattered down. Out in the harbour, the crew of one of the local trading smacks jumped to the conclusion that war had been declared. The 'shot' whizzed through the shrouds of their vessel, but why the mangled remains of a cat should have hurtled themselves through the open companion-way of their cabin, was a mystery beyond their solution.

In the town consternation soon gave way to investigation, and the discovery of a cannon resting peacefully a long way behind its platform, revealed the cause of the alarm. With the coming of daylight, the damage done could be assessed, and it was no mean damage that this terrific bang had done, for, among other things, the chimney-head, between the properties now occupied by Messrs J. & J. Tod and Mr Laurence Robertson, at that time the home of the Sutherland family—Brothers Tom, Andrew and James and Sister Barbara—was so badly shaken and cracked that it was in danger of collapsing. Robert Ridland, blacksmith, was engaged, for the sum of £12, to secure it, and this he did with great straps of iron bands which stood so well that they remained for all to see till 1933 when the chimney-head was rebuilt.

A hue and cry was raised after the perpetrators of this outrage, but, before they could be found out, the 'boys' had deemed it safer to make themselves scarce, and none was brought to justice.

Two of the lads were sons of well known Lerwick citizens. One of these was a high-spirited youth who was known to have taken a leading part in many of the more daring ploys. He was the first to be suspected as the ringleader, and, only an hour or two after the firing of the cannon, the police visited his home and found a very 'innocent' young man sound asleep in his bed. The very fact that he was in bed in the early hours of a New Year's morning, was quite sufficient to convict him in the eyes of all who knew him, but, for the moment, there was not sufficient evidence forthcoming to warrant his arrest.

With so serious a charge hanging over their heads and the risk that the police might be able to bring it home to them, both these lads deemed it advisable to leave Shetland, and both ultimately reached New Zealand. The Authorities, believing that the real culprits had fled, allowed the matter to drop.

It is of interest to record that the 'innocent' sleeper of that New Year's morning made good and attained a very high position in his adopted home, but, till the day of his death, he never forgot the 'bang' with which he and his squad ushered in the year 1861.

CHAPTER IX.

MORE TALES AND COMMENTS.

A law student, swotting-up for his finals, would search Erskine's *Principles* in vain for any mention of the Tar Act, but, had he lived in Lerwick when Tar-barrelling was in vogue, he would have required no instruction as to what it was or in the method of its administration.

Woe betide the luckless merchant who had, wittingly or unwittingly, trodden on the toes of the guizers. He was invariably condemned, without a hearing, to have the Tar Act administered on him. It has already been related how Mr Robertson of the Trance suffered at the hands of the Tar-barrellers. His sentence was executed in the form of blazing tar, but, in the following incident, the more usual form of liquid tar was used.

The victim of this tale was William Laurenson, a grand-uncle of Mr P. Bruce Laurenson, the present secretary of the Up-Helly-Aa Committee. Mr Laurenson resided in the house above his shop in Commercial Street so long occupied by his nephew, the late Peter Laurenson. He had the misfortune to incur the displeasure of the 'boys', and was condemned to suffer the pains and penalties of the Tar Act.

One of the guizers quietly gave old William the hint that the 'boys' had decided, that night, to tar his shop windows.

William thanked him for the information, and determined, there and then, that their reception would be a right warm one. Arming himself with his shotgun he sat up all night waiting for the assault which, however, did not materialise.

Next day he met his informant, who assured him that the tarring had been planned for the previous night but that some of the 'boys' had had other ploys in hand, and that it had been decided that it would be carried out the following night. William spent another weary vigil with the same result. Again his informer persuaded him that for various reasons the vile designs of the 'boys' had been postponed for another twentyfour hours. Another fruitless night-watch was kept, and, tired out with three successive sleepless nights, William decided that the information, so gratuitously given, was without foundation and that he need no longer deprive himself of much-needed rest.

The following night, while he was making up for lost sleep, sundry sack-covered figures might have been seen, in the small hours, gathering round 159, Commercial Street. They made sure that there was no prowling policeman in the vicinity, and proceeded with brush and tar to paint the doors, windows and even the walls with a thick, shiny coat of tar. The Tar Act had been administered.

When William awoke next morning, it was to find his shop and house wearing mourning of the deepest dye. Recrimination and dire threats of vengeance might relieve his feelings, but they would not remove the tar, so there was nothing for it but to turn-to with the assistance of his shopboy, and clean up. A few gallons of paraffin and innumerable clouts were needed before the premises were made presentable, and William's temper was not improved by the passers-by who stopped to gaze at his labours, nor by the facetious remarks of people who 'ought to have known better'. It is said that one young man had the temerity to ask for the loan of William's shotgun, but the very forcible answer he got, made it clear that he was more likely to get its contents if he did not clear off.

By the time, however, that the shop and house were once more in a presentable condition, William's anger had evaporated, and, in discussing the outrage with a crony, he was heard to express regret that he had not stuck it out for one more night : "By Jiminy ! I wud hae tarred dem, da deevils". Little did he know that there was a traitor within his gates and that, so long as he remained on guard, no administrator of the Tar Act would dare approach his premises.

The next tale is of an amusing episode concerning the Special constables and a Tar-barrel.

On one Up-Helly-Aa night, during Chief Constable MacKay's tenure of office, a Tar-barrel with its attendant crew and crowd of guizers had passed over the Street and had just reached a point opposite Dr Pole's house which, at that time, stood on the site now occupied by the north end of the Post Office. Here its further progress was barred by a squad of Specials under the leadership of the Chief. As usual, when a capture could not be avoided, the squad and the guizers dropped the chain and melted into the crowd, and their places were taken by the Specials who, in accordance with the usual practice, had to haul it on to some open space or on to the beach where it could burn out without risk of damage.

On this occasion, the Cockstool was the nearest open spot, and towards it the Specials were ordered to drag the blazing Tar-barrel. The guizers and a crowd of onlookers stood by to watch their efforts and to encourage them with sarcastic advice. The Specials pulled and pulled again but the Tar-barrel, with its boiling, spluttering tar and terrific heat, seemed rooted to the street, while overhead the thick, oily cloud of smoke grew dense and yet more dense. The Tar-barrel was not an unduly

heavy cne and the force of Specials was large, so it can only
be concluded that it was want of inclination rather than want
of man-power which was the cause of their failure to move it.
"Old MacKay" shouted to them to pull, and the spectators
added their quota of caustic exhortations, but still the
Tar-barrel held its ground.

The onlookers were now thoroughly enjoying themselves,
but not so Dr Pole, whose house was in danger of being
burned down.   Already, blisters were forming on the
paintwork, and indeed, in some places the paint was beginning
to run and panes of glass to crack.   The position was getting
serious; the Doctor was frantic, but apparently, pull as hard
as they could, the Specials could not move that Tar-barrel.
The situation had now reached a point at which it was too
dangerous to permit of further delay, and the Chief, realising
that he was beaten, appealed to the guizers to get the tar-barrel
into safer quarters.   They were nothing loth, and, with yells
of victory, speedily acceded to his request : a few minutes
later, the Tar-barrel was merrily burning itself out in front of
the Tolbooth.

Mention has so often been made of the Cockstool, that
it is worth while to pause a little and give a more detailed
description cf this favourite spot for 'burnings'.

The Cockstool, itself, was a flattish, humpy rock on the
beach below the Tolbooth.   By reason of its proximity to this
rock, the space in front of the Tolbooth became known by
the same name, and the house on Commercial Street, just north
of this building, is still known as the Cockstool Shop.   In
those days, the whole foundations of the Tolbooth were on
the same level as the present Esplanade.   One can still see
the door of the cellars in the north wall, but the windows of
these cellars, which were in front of the building, have long
disappeared as the result of heightening the street.   So, when
you think of the Cockstool of olden days, you must try to

visualise it as a very steep, flagged close or square with a passage leading down to the beach past the north gable of the Tolbooth, and a narrow roadway on the south side which was really the landward end of Hay's Pier.

After Tar-barrelling had been prohibited, the youth of the town still found outlet for practical jokes and pranks during the holiday season. The late R. B. Hunter, Agent of the Union Bank, was an ardent guizer in his younger days, and, as such, took many a leading part in the Yuletide ploys. He used to take a delight in telling a story against himself of how some of his own chums played a trick on him one morning during the festive season.

Mr Hunter's home was in the Burgh Road, and on going out one morning on his way to the Bank, where he was then an apprentice, he was amazed to find a number of scavengers' barrows standing neatly in a row in the front garden. Considerable trouble had been taken to make the display artistic, for each barrow stood upright, facing the road, with its handles stuck well into the flower beds, while on either side, as if at attention, stood the broom and the shovel. The fact that, already, passers-by were stopping to admire this new form of garden decoration and were making kind enquiries as to where he got the seeds for such exotic plants, did not appeal to R.B.'s sense of humour at that hour of the morning, and his temper was not improved by fervent appeals not to uproot such elegant shrubs.

Later in the day, Chief Constable MacKay, who was also head of the scavenging department, interviewed him. In his deep, slow, gruff voice he enquired, "Robert, do you know anything about my scavengers' barrows?" "Yes, that I do", replied Robert with some heat. "You'll find them at the back of our house, and you had better see that they are removed as quickly as possible". "Aha! Robert", slowly remarked the old Chief, "it would be *thy* boat that was up-ended on her side and tied across my door this morning, so that I could not get out until I got some passers-by to untie her and haul her to one side. You had better take her away".

R.B. at once made his way to the Chief's house at Hillhead, and, sure enough, it was his own boat which his chums had taken from her winter noost[14] at the Craigie Stane below Quendale House, and dragged all the way up to the Hillhead in order to barricade 'Old MacKay' in, while they collected the barrows, shovels and brooms for the adornment of Robert's home.

The narrowness of the Street was responsible for yet another ploy indulged in by the youth of old Lerwick. It took the form of raising a barricade across the street, and then, from a point of vantage, watching the results. The late Alex. Ratter, Curator of the Library, told of one such ploy in which he was one of the leading spirits.

Just south of the Market Cross was the narrowest part in the Street, and near-by there was an open enclosure on the shore in which large piles of empty boxes and crates were stored to await shipment. One evening, young Ratter and his chums were playing around this spot when one of them suggested that it would be a good ploy to block the street with the boxes. To these young rascals, to suggest was to act, and soon the boxes were being passed up as fast as the boys could handle them. Quickly the barricade began to rise, and had reached about five feet in height when the florid, angry face of 'Old MacKay' made its appearance on the other side. "Boys, boys!" he shouted, "Stop this nonsense at once. No, no! this is going too far. I'll have you all in Court. Stop it! I say". By this time the spirit of devilment had got too good a hold on the boys, and, regardless of the dire threats from

---

[14]Noost:—An excavation in the sea-banks where a boat is secured for the winter.

the fast disappearing head on the other side, they continued to pile up the boxes until the street was completely blocked.

Wheeled traffic had ceased for the day but there were still many pedestrians who wished to go north or south, and this could only be done by making a détour up one lane and down another or, alternatively, going round by the beach which, here-abouts, was an unsavoury spot in daylight but an unspeakable place to traverse after dark.

The folks who had suffered annoyance from the barricade, were justly indignant, and complaint after complaint was made to the police. Next day, the Chief entered the office of the *Shetland Times* and demanded an interview with 'young Ratter' who was serving his apprenticeship in that establishment. When he had answered the summons, the Chief ponderously addressed him thus :—"Alexander Ratter, you have gone over the score this time. The lieges have been very much annoyed and will not tolerate it. I must make a Court case of it, and you and the other boys will have to appear. No, no ! I cannot let you off : the lieges are very much annoyed", and then, as if to soften the blow, "but I'll try to get you off, seeing that you have not been in the Court before".

Sure enough, all the boys were summoned to appear before the Magistrates, and were duly charged with obstructing the highway, etc. They pled guilty, but 'old MacKay' was as good as his word, for, after reciving a severe lecture from the Bench on their 'most unwarranted behaviour', they got off with an admonishment and were discharged. It says much for the acknowledged fairness of this stern old man, that not a single boy bore him the least ill will for his having 'made a Court case of it'.

CHAPTER X.

THE present generation would have great difficulty in visualising the Lerwick of the Sixties and Seventies— no Esplanade, no Victoria Pier, no Herring Market and no Town Hall or County Buildings. There were a few houses on the Hillhead but practically none to the westward. Instead of a broad highway below Fort Charlotte, the road, such as it was, wound its way along the banks above the beach round the foot of the rock. From there southwards, built out into the sea were many houses with their lodberries[15], where, in addition to lawful merchandise, many a good keg of brandy and sack of tobacco were landed without paying the Queen's dues.

The reader will get a better idea of the town in those days if he will picture in his mind the area now enclosed by a line drawn from the north end of Commercial Street, through Charlotte Lane and westward to the Burgh Road, down the east side of the Burgh Road on to Freefield, and thence, following the seashore round by the Northness, back to our starting point at the foot of the 'Garrison Close'.

Within this area, the only buildings then erected, other

---

[15]Lodberry:—An enclosed yard, having a sea gate where boats could load or discharge goods.

than Fort Charlotte, were the Old Mill and Millhouse just below the present Fort Road in Mill Lane; the Gas Works and Gas Works Cottage; two houses and two cottages in the present Northness Road; two houses and two cottages on the Northness fishing station; a small cottage in Freefield Park; the double house at the top of Freefield Road; the Freefield business premises and the smithy belonging to the late John Brown.

The Burgh Road might well have been named 'The Porker Prom', so many were the pig-styes on both sides of the road right down to the Slates. One can hardly realise, nowadays, the enormous number of pigs which were kept. Mention has been made of those in Whisky Lane, but here, there and all over the town, were pig-styes, with further colonies on the outskirts along both the North and South Roads; in fact, there was scarcely a family which did not keep a pig or pigs for home consumption or 'to pay the rent'.

At Freefield, Garthspool and Skibbadock, lived most of the folks who worked at the Docks—carpenters, sailmakers, coopers, cod-splitters, fishermen, etc. They formed a small compact community by themselves; the stores at the Docks supplied practically all their needs, and, broadly speaking, they had little intercourse with the town. During the Yule festivities the 'Docks Boys' were known as the 'Northerners' while the 'Town Boys' were called the 'Southerners'. It has been suggested that the American Civil War, then in progress, was responsible for these names.

The open area between the town and the Docks, described above, divided the Southerners and the Northerners into two opposing factions, and the rivalry between the two resulted in many a tussle and hand-to-hand fight. With the bridging over of this 'no man's land' with roads and buildings, the old enmities have disappeared, but even to this day, the

E

'Docks Boys' have their accredited representatives on the Up-Helly-Aa Committee.

In the earlier days of Tar-barrelling, the Northerners were just as enthusiastic Barrellers as the Southerners, and they invaded the Street along with their supporters just in the same way as did the 'Town Boys'. It was an unwritten but, none the less, inexorable law, that, once a Tar-barrel had been set on its course through the Street, it must hold that course, come what might, until it reached the Cockstool, where it was turned about and returned in the same determined manner to the foot of the Garrison Close. Here it was turned about again and so back and fore it went until it was time to make it into a bon-fire.

The turning round of a Tar-barrel was a scene of great excitement. Having reached the Cockstool, there was enacted a turning movement having nothing in common with the present-day one which takes place in King Harald Street during the Up-Helly-Aa torchlight procession. What was lost in the way of military orderliness was more than made up for in a scene of barbaric disorderliness.

As soon as the leader of the squad deemed that the Tar-barrel had sufficient room to turn, he would yell out at the top of his voice, "Sweep her! sweep her!". The guizers on the drag chain would take up the cry, the crowd would join in, and, with everyone yelling, "Sweep her! sweep her!", round would swing the long double line of guizers, jostling the crowd back and getting in one another's way in a glorious mix-up, till the chain tightened and jerked them back into order again. As the fore-end of the tar-barrel began to swing round, sack-covered figures worked furiously at the stern. Oars and pieces of wood were used to lever it round, and gradually the bows would be set on their northward course, and off the procession would go again.

Commercial Street, as we know it today, is a narrow,

tortuous street, but it is a broad thoroughfare compared with
what it was sixty or seventy years ago. There were, at that
time, two extremely narrow places : one, known as The Roost,
was at the foot of Bank Lane ; the other, the narrower of the
two, just to the south of the Market Cross, was situated
between the shop, now occupied by Mr J. R. White, and a
small, low-eaved grocery store which stood on what is now
the street in front of Messrs Anderson & Company's premises.

At these points there was just enough room to allow a
Shetland country cart to pass, and on both sides could be seen
grooves in the walls caused by the wheel axles of carts which
failed to make a middle passage. It sometimes happened,
and by no means always by accident, that the Northerners
with their Tar-barrel, preceded by the long drag chain manned
by as many yelling and cheering guizers as could get a handgrip
on it, would enter The Roost and attempt to pass a Southerner
Tar-barrel going in the opposite direction, and likewise manned
by a similar yelling, cheering mob.

Just try to imagine the scene. There are the two long,
double lines of guizers forcing their way past each other through
a five or six foot passage, each dragging behind it a great
flaming sledge, almost as wide as the street itself, and anything
from ten to twenty feet long. With shouts of defiance and
insults, the opposing crews force their way through, and, as
the two Tar-barrels almost meet, the guizers next the bows
jump and scramble clear. Yells, shouts and curses rend the
air. The police are swept aside as they try to delay the
progress of one side or the other to allow the Tar-barrels to
pass while there is yet room, but they might as well adjure
the enclosing walls to fall apart. The Tar-barrels crash
together, and boiling blazing tar is scattered in all directions :
the tug-of-war commences, and now between the combatants
there is a veritable inferno of fire and scorching heat. Neither
side relaxes for an instant : the curses, shouts and yells grow

louder. The excited onlookers yell encouragement to their own partisans cr equally to both sides. It is pandemonium let loose.

The Specials no longer even attempt to restore order, and, if truth be told, they are probably thoroughly enjoying themselves, as, more than likely, it is not so long since they, themselves, were active participants in just such a *mêlée*. Tempers break loose and fists come into play. Masked figures hit out indiscriminately at other masked figures, but still the struggle for supremacy goes on.

There were only two ways out of the *impasse*. Either one side, more strongly manned than the other, forced the opposing Tar-barrel far enough back to allow the other to clear it, or one Tar-barrel was forced up and over the other, leaving behind a fiery furnace on the street for the Specials to deal with. Burns, black eyes and bleeding mouths were common after such a battle, and yet, strange to relate, no ill will was borne, and the fighting fiends of the early morning would be the best of friends the following day, and would boast and chaff each other about the grand time they had had when they met in The Roost.

This was a trait which strikes one as very remarkable, and which went to prove that it was the game that mattered and nothing else. There were, in fact, lads among the Northerners, employed in the same workshops as lads from the Southerners, who, at all other times, were the greatest of pals but who, when it came to a fight between the two factions, would hammer each other in deadly earnest, and yet be the closest of friends again next day.

So much did this fighting spirit in the mass prevail, that it was no uncommon thing during the festivities, with no Tar-barrels to inflame their passions, for two bands of Northerners and Southerners to club together and subscribe a few shillings to buy an old rowing boat which was beyond repair. Except for the usual bantering boasts as to what one side would do to the other, the boat was hauled up to the Street in quite an orderly manner. Arrived there, one band would cluster round the gunwales at the bow, and the other would take station at the stern. When all were in position, they would start the contest; one faction trying to pull the boat northwards while the other did its best to pull it southwards. Before long the temperature began to rise, and,

as the old boat came to bits, so did their tempers. The same old shouts, yells and curses which excited them at the Tar-barrel would re-echo in the street; the boat would be forgotten and a free fight ensue. They had attained their object.

On one occasion the two factions, having made up their minds to have a boat-pulling contest, either from sheer devilment or want of cash, stole an ancient boat belonging to an old man, named Innes Tait, who for many years acted as boatman to the Dutch busses lying out in the harbour. By the time the contest was over, there was little of the old boat left, but, later, when their heads had cooled, the 'boys' realised the injury they had done to old Innes, and decided that they must recompense him for the loss of his boat.

It so happened that, just then, there was a fairly good boat for sale at the Custom House, so on the day following the fight the erstwhile deadly combatants clubbed together and raised sufficient money among them to purchase it. Old Innes was highly delighted with the turn of events, for the old man was already mourning the loss of his boat and, what was more vital to him, his only means of making a meagre livelihood.

The years passed on, and for various reasons the ranks of
the Northerners were thinned. Work at the Docks became
scarcer, and the young men had to go to sea or emigrate.
Some went to the Colonies, while others took jobs 'i' da
sooth', but the death knell of the Northerners was sounded
when the Colvin boys, their leaders in many a hard fought
fight, left the Islands.   With their departure, the fighting
forces of the Northerners began to weaken and finally
disappeared.   Tar-barrelling, thereafter, became exclusively
a town affair.

From the foregoing incidents, it might be inferred that it
was only when Northerner met Southerner that the tussles for
supremacy were fought. This was not so. There was a
similar rivalry between squads residing at the north and south
ends of the town, the dividing line being the Baker's Close
(Mounthooly Street), but it mattered not who the principal
antagonists were, the unwritten law prevailed—no giving way
and no retreat when Barrellers met and fought the
time-honoured Battle of The Roost.

And now, before bidding farewell to the Tar-barrels,
let our 'Counsel for the Defence' pay his tribute to that
outstanding figure of his youth—Chief Constable MacKay.

"He was a grand old man whom we both loved and
feared. If I close my eyes, I can still see his short, square
figure and ruddy whiskers, and hear the thump, thump of his
stick on the paving stones when he spotted us at some youthful
prank.

"As boys, any old night, during the Yule festivities,
was a Tar-barrel night. Could we but get hold of an old
kishie or box, we made our Tar-barrel, and up and down
the lanes we would run until someone shouted 'Here's Old
MacKay' !, and, leaving our Tar-barrel to its fate, off we
would scamper and seek refuge wherever it might be found.

"Later, when we had grown up a bit, we would delight

in teasing the old man. A dark night was necessary when we indulged in this ploy, and the lanes were darksome places in those days. Perhaps half-a-dozen of us would start annoying him, in the way only boys can, until at last he would chase after us, and, as we ran, first one boy and then another would disappear into some dark corner until 'Old MacKay' had no one left to chase.

"But the old man was no mean runner, and occasionally a boy would be caught, and, there and then, a juvenile court would be held on the spot with 'Old MacKay' as Prosecutor, Judge and Executioner. The verdict was always 'Guilty'. A few welts with his stick on what ever spot was most vulnerable, a series of yells, and justice had been done—till next time. He was very gruff in his manner, but I do believe that he enjoyed the fun as much as we did. Yes, a grand old man".

And so goodbye to Tar-barrelling nights, but, as already told, the dying embers of the bon-fire marked but the beginning of the revels.

CHAPTER XI.

GUIZING.

THE normal number in a Guizing Squad rarely exceeded six or seven, one of whom would be the fiddler, and he was not supplied with that luxury of later days—a fiddle-box carrier.

In those days, the guizers were all entertained in private houses, and larger squads would have over-crowded the room set out to receive them. Incidentally, the Guizing Squad was composed of the same individuals who formed the Tar-barrel Squad; the latter were augmented by other guizers but immediately reverted to their original number after the 'burning'.

At 1 or 1.30 a.m., a Tar-barrel squad was the most disreputable crowd imaginable : splashed with tar, begrimed with soot and smoke, and soaked with perspiration, they were not fit to meet, much less dance with, the girls who awaited them in the various houses.

After the 'burning', the first necessity was to get home and out of Tar-barrelling dresses, then, after much scrubbing and washing, the proper guizing dresses were donned, and it is certain that, after all the excitement of the previous few hours, right glad they were to get rid of the grime, and replace it with the sweet smell of good yellow soap. There were always some final touches or adjustments to be made to the guizing costumes, and it would be well on to three o'clock before the squad would be ready to sally forth to enjoy the fun and dancing which would continue till 9 a.m. or even later.

In spite of the glories of the modern Up-Helly-Aa, the guizing dresses of sixty or more years ago would not concede one iota to those of today, either in ingenuity or colourfulness. Each member of the squad made his own costume, although, occasionally, it did happen that a guizer was hopeless with needle and thread. In such a case, the assistance of a sister or girl friend was invoked, under solemn oath of secrecy, to do the stitching for him.

The following is a description of a dress in which a squad 'went out' in the late Seventies. The squad represented devils from the nether regions, and, with a touch of sardonic humour, a gentleman in clerical dress was the only member who did not wear the reputed garb of His Satanic Majesty.

Starting from the feet and working upwards, a pair of long socks was drawn over the rivlins[16], then over the socks came tight-fitting woollen pants, the waistband of which was covered by the bottom hem of a slip which was drawn over the head and had sleeves down to the wrists. This foundation, so to speak, was dyed jet black. Attached to the ankles and running up the outside of the legs and body, and down the inside of the arms to the little fingers, were black gauze wings. The ribs of the wings radiated fan-shaped from the ankles to a scalloped edge, and on the end of each rib was fixed a scarf's[17] claw.

When the arms were flexed sideways and upwards, there was a lifelike likeness to the wings of devils as depicted in old woodcuts. Of course, no devil appeared without a tail,

---

[16]Rivlins:—Raw cowhide shoes.
[17]Scarf:—The local name given to a cormorant or shag without differentiation.

and those for this dress were made from long flexible springs
which were kept in position by being rigidly fixed along the
wearer's spine. The long, tapering, padded tail was painted
black at the root and gradually merged into a vivid scarlet
at the point. The tip was finished off with a conventional
barb, just above which was attached a rattle. Most of the
squad managed by criss-crossing to give the tail a scaly skin.

Over the head and neck was drawn a black, close-fitting
cowl with dumpy red horns on either side of the brow. Around
the eyeholes there was a fierce red, while above were slanting,
tipped eyebrows. Just to complete the sinister appearance of
the eyes, the eyelids were painted white. The nose was
long and hooked, dull red at the base merging to vermilion
at the tip.

The jaws were hinged and displayed a set of sharp
pointed fangs, while from the mouth protruded a flaming red,
forked tongue made from a piece of spring steel which, in the
case of one member, was purloined from his mother's stays.
All over the face were whitish and red blotches which were
made by the simple process of melting down red and white
indiarubber. The teeth and fangs were likewise moulded from
white rubber. To complete the *ensemble,* each member
carried a sort of trident with vicious looking prongs, so, what
with jaws clamping, the forked tongue vibrating, and the
barbed tail swinging about in all directions, the whole outfit
presented a truly fearsome appearance.

This dress, with the exception of the knitted garments,
was made from beginning to end by the members of the squad.
There were minor variations according to the fancy and skill
of the individual, but these enhanced, rather than took away
from, the general effect. The making of the dress was done
in the evenings and in any odd hours available, and the job
took several weeks to complete, but one member has left it
on record that the making of this particular costume not only

invoked an intense interest on the part of the squad, but actually provided them with almost as much fun as the wearing of it on Yule and New Year's mornings. What with cinemas, badminton, darts, billiards and bridge, the youth of today could scarcely find time for such efforts or go to so much trouble to attain effects.

Another fine individual effort was that of a youth who 'went out' as a Red Indian. He made his robe from the skins of the grey scarf from which he had plucked the long feathers, thus leaving a soft, furry grey down which completely deceived more than one envious lady into thinking that he was wearing a beautiful grey fur. The scalp he fashioned from an unplucked skin of the green scarf.

Further descriptions of squads and their dresses will be given later, but meantime, let us get back to 3 a.m. on the night of the 'burning'.

The last titivation having been made and dresses donned, the squad would set off on a round of visitation. A dozen or so houses would be 'open', and it was a point of honour on the part of all guizers that visits must be made to the greatest number possible. Each 'open' house set apart a room, usually the kitchen for the reception of the guizers, and, there, awaiting them, were the dancing lasses and some elder folks who were, mostly, just as keen to join in a dance as the younger ones.

Refreshments were provided—currant loaf, home-made scones, biscuits and cakes which were washed down with cups of tea and coffee, and mugs of home-made drinks. Sandwiches were not then in vogue, although they became very popular in later years. For those who liked something with more of a kick in it, there was, in most houses, a drop of the 'best', and with the 'best' at two and sixpence a bottle, or less if it had not paid the Queen's dues, there was not an undue strain on the household purse.

When the squad were approaching a house, they formed up and, sometimes, struck up a song like "John Brown's Body". The words might be the original or parodied into some doggerel to suit the characters represented by the squad, but the more usual form of entry was to troop in with every member yelling out a long-drawn 'Ah-e-e-e' which rose and fell according to the amount of breath left in their lungs.

In order to make room for the squad's antics and the dancing, the room, with its bare boarded or flagged floor, had already been cleared of most of the furniture. Round the walls were chairs and forms for the guests, while, seated near the fire, were the old folks whose dancing days were done but who could not resist sitting up to join in the fun.

'Dancing days were done' did we say? Not a bit of it ! Time and again Granfedder and Granny too, whose toes would keep on tap, tap, tapping out the tune, would be coaxed on to the floor for a Shetland Reel, and, with flushed, happy faces, would stamp and reel with the best.

By the side of the fire, stood a huge tea kettle, whose contents were kept up by just adding a spoonful more tea leaves and more boiling water. They liked their brew strong and black. On the dresser in a corner or on a table in the next room, were stacked heaped plates of provender.

Entry into the house was according to the character of the guizing dress worn, either slow and dignified or frolicsome and sprightly. The squad of 'devils', already described, went in jumping and prancing as if bewitched, while the poor parson was jolted out of what was supposed to be a solemn and dignified gait by sundry prods in the rear from their forked spears.

Masks were never doffed unless the identity of the guizers was established, and not even then if the identification was confined to only one or two. It was the height of ambition of every real guizer to go through the three Guizing Nights of

Yule, New Year and Up-Helly-Aa without being recognised. Hosts and friends did not feel they had been slighted, if a squad could visit and leave a house unidentified : in fact, the non-recognition of a guizer was a great asset to him when, later, he met his host and his friends, and continued to mystify them as to who their visitors really were.

Having made their entry and carried out any pre-arranged antics, the members of the squad would, individually, start an 'aff-lay'[18] with their hosts and the guests. A real expert in the art of aff-lay was a joy to listen to, as, without rehearsal or even a moment's hesitation, he would, from behind the security of his mask, recount the eccentricities of his family, but more especially of Osla, his wife, 'da trooker'[19], the weather, the crops, the fishing, his lumbago, his coortin' days, the perversity of his grice[20], and the failure of his hens to lay eggs and his proposed plans to remedy this state of affairs.

If his listener happened to be a Town Councillor, the current affairs of the burgh were pungently dealt with in a way that would have been impossible in public debate; if a teacher or a head-master, the aff-layer was invariably an old pupil, and the merits, or rather the demerits, 'o' dis modren eddicashun' would be compared with that of his youth which was always ages ago, although, actually, the aff-layer might have little more than left school. Then, more in sorrow than in anger, would follow a discourse on the teacher's unrighteous punishments of a 'puir innocent bairn'. And so on the aff-lay would go, ranging from Greenland whalers or 'castin' peats' to 'sockit pilticks'[21], 'liver muggies'[22] and 'stap'[23].

---

[18]Aff-lay :—Literally, a laying-off of words.
[19]Trooker :—Bad woman, vixen.
[20]Grice :—Pig.
[21]Sookit pilticks :—Air-cured young saithe or coalfish.
[22]Liver Muggies :—Fish liver cooked in the stomach of the fish.
[23]Stap :—Fish liver and the flesh from the head, minced together, cooked and seasoned.

No subject under the sun came amiss, but the greatest fun of all was when his *vis-à-vis* was as good at the aff-lay as himself. Then, indeed, it was a battle of repartee till, with the two principals still 'laying-off' to one another in apparent seriousness and solemnity, they became the centre of a hilarious, laughing throng which crowded round them to enjoy a treat which would have been hard to beat by professional cross-chat comedians.

The aff-lay over, or still being carried on by individual members, someone calls for a dance, the fiddler strikes up a tune, without ceremony the guizers seize their partners, and, accompanied by the rhythmical tap, tap or rather stamp of the feet, they hooch and skirl their way through a Shetland reel till the music stops, and amid more skirling and wriggling, the guizers embrace their partners and perform the final rite of 'Kiss da lasses'. The fact that the kissing was done with masks on, only added to the fun. Incidentally, it was an invariable rule that, provided the guizer was not objectionable, which was sometimes the case, no lady could refuse to dance with him unless she had some good excuse to offer, such as over-tiredness or duties in connection with the catering.

The Shetland reel, although the prime favourite, was, by no means, the only dance indulged in : there were Foula, Eightsome and Foursome reels, Waltzes, Polkas, Schottisches and, even sometimes, that latest importation 'fae da Sooth', the Quadrille.

It was heavy going, and in the confined space of the small rooms, even with the doors and windows open, the guizers perspired profusely behind their masks till the sweat blinded their eyes, and it was impossible to get even temporary relief by the use of a handkerchief. But youth does not worry about such trifles, and, with masks thrown back, they could always get cooled down on their way to the next house.

While one lot of dancers occupied the floor, the hostess

and her assistants busied themselves with handing round refreshments to the others. The refreshment period was a critical one for the guizer, as, if he had not already been spotted and doffed his mask, he had the difficult job of 're-fuelling' without being detected, and feeding-time was the favourite opportunity for the ladies to become intensely inquisitive. Often it was impossible to eat without removing the mask, and in such a case the only thing to be done was to secret some provender about the dress and consume it outside.

It was a recognised custom that the same members of a squad would go out as such in the squad guizing dress on Yule and New Year. The same dress was worn on both occasions, and practically the same houses visited. As far as possible, there were variations in the antics and aff-lay according to individual skill and experience, but on Up-Helly-Aa night there was a complete change of programme. The squad dress was discarded, and each member was at liberty to dress himself according to his fancy. On Up-Helly-Aa night, too, members were no longer bound to conform to any prearranged programme, and the individual was at liberty to indulge in his own particular style of play-acting. As a general rule, the original squad still kept together, but it was no uncommon practice for one or two members to break away and link up with another squad. This was usually done if the squad had been identified at Yule or New Year; the more unlikely the combination of individuals, the less chance there was of again being detected.

Then might be seen the old-time Skudler, Grulik or Skekler[24] crowned with his intricately plaited, tall straw head-dress, at first glance somewhat resembling a bishop's

---

[24]Skudler, Grulik, Skekler:—The old name for guizers or maskers. 'Gruliks' and 'Skeklers' was the general name given to guizers, while 'Skudler' was the name more appropriate to the leader. Edmondston gives 'Skudler' as "The master of ceremonies or leader of a band of maskers".

mitre, and attired in a straw cape and petticoat; all survivals of the days when the humble crofter had no means or opportunity to procure the latest fashions, and had to rely on the products of his rig[25] and his own art as a weaver of kishies[26] and flakkies[27].

Some wonderful creations were produced. The straw hat rose high above the head in twisted ropes which ended in rings and spirals tied together with coloured ribbons whose long, flowing ends gave a note of gaiety to the whole dress. The cape over the shoulders had arm-holes through which the arms were thrust, and its lower edge covered the waist-band of the petticoat which extended to below the knees. Very occasionally, the legs were trousered in straw, but the arms were invariably left free. A home-made mask completed the costume.

One of the most popular characterisations on Up-Helly-Aa, and one which never palled or grew stale, was that of a family group led by an old country woman, almost always bent double, who was accompanied by her rather insignificant looking husband and a son or daughter or both. The old lady would have on her back a kishie filled with brünies[28], bannocks, eggs, a lump of butter and, perhaps, a flagon of blaand[29] or bleddik[30], while, in a covered square basket carried in her hand, there would be a fowl, usually dead but sometimes, very audibly, alive.

The general idea in portraying this act, if one may be allowed to apply such a term to an Up-Helly-Aa 'ploy', was to represent a country family on a visit to the town on pleasure

---

[25]Rig:—The arable land on a croft is divided into sections called 'rigs' for the purpose of rotation of crops.
[26]Kishie:—A creel made of straw.
[27]Flakki:—A straw mat used in winnowing corn.
[28]Brüni:—Very thick round oat cake.
[29]Blaand:—The liquid left behind after boiling water has been poured on buttermilk and the resulting solids (kirn milk) have been removed.
[30]Bleddik:—Buttermilk.

and business bent, and one has to bear in mind that, in those days, journeys to the town were only possible on foot or by boat, so that a visit to the Capital was a real event in their lives, hence the keen interest in all that they saw.   In trying to give a picture of this 'family' guizing, one can only touch

GUIZERS VISITING.

on the wealth of fun and humour which was unfolded.   The masks were carefully chosen—the old lady's, sharp-featured and alert; the husband's, old and rather vacant; the son's, feckless, and the daughter's usually simpering.   Imagine, then, that the 'open' house is the town, and substitute the pictures, furniture, etc., for the shop windows.

In walks the family, led by the old lady and her husband, followed by the son and daughter.   Round the room they saunter seemingly quite oblivious to the presence of anyone else ; here, a picture catches their eyes, and they halt to gaze and admire it ; there, a piece of furniture claims their attention, while they critically appraise its value or its usefulness ; again,

F

it may be a vase of flowers that calls forth "Isna' dat da boanie?"

The entry made, the aff-lay commences. Osla (Ursula)—the old lady was nearly always 'Osla', while, just as often, her husband was 'Lowrie' (Laurence)—approaches a host or a guest and starts to sell her wares. As each article is produced from her kishie, she holds it up in front of her prospective customer's face, and asks "What tinks du o' dat"?, and immediately proceeds to extol its excellence and superiority to anything to be bought in the town. If the would-be consumer is an adept, the ensuing discussion gives Osla the opportunity to indulge in serio-comical repartee which draws peals of laughter from the spectators. When the lump of butter is produced, Osla carefully turns back the paper wrapper, deftly scrapes off a sample with the back of her thumb nail, and holds it up to her customer's mouth with the exhortation, "Taste du dat. Du niver tastit its better". And so on.

During all the time that Osla was trying to sell her wares, Lowrie would stand by her side, hardly uttering a word beyond, perhaps at suitable intervals, "Yea, yea! dat is so", while the son and daughter carried on an aff-lay in another part of the room. All at once, a guest notices the poor, miserable object by her side, and turns to Osla with the question "An' wha micht dis be"? to which would come the prompt reply, "O' yon! dat's Lowrie; puir aamus[31] ting dat he is. Yea, yea! dat's Lowrie; we wir mairried in eichteen fortynine bit ———" and then would follow a full recital of Lowrie's shortcomings both as a man and a husband, who was for ever afflicted with 'screwmatics', 'plumbago', 'peumonie' or whatever fantastic complaint came into Osla's mind.

---

[31]Aamus:—Probably connected with the English word 'alms'. As used here, 'deserving' might express the meaning.

Having introduced Lowrie, Osla would call over her son, Gibbie (Gilbert), and her daughter, Leebie (Elizabeth), and they, in turn, would be introduced, and their facial and other peculiarities fully described with much wealth of detail. On the type of masks they wore and any incongruities in their dresses—and they were many—would greatly depend the scope of Osla's descriptions. Her tongue would never rest nor would she ever be at a loss for a pertinent answer to the most personal questions. The whole inner secrets of the family would be laid bare, their 'coortins', their prospects and so on *ad infinitum*, but, throughout it all, whether selling eggs or retailing the shortcomings of her husband and family, Osla remained the dominant, forceful old dame from the top of her bugled lace bonnet to the soles of her elastic-sided boots[32].

Dutchmen, Jack Tars, Soldiers, Chinamen, Red Indians, prim old ladies, simpering young girls and any other characters that the guizers' imagination could evolve, would be out on Up-Helly-Aa night. No need now for a squad to work as a team; each individual guizer could make his own style of fun, or a few might band together and make up a party representing whalers, sailors home from foreign parts or some local body, but it was mainly on Up-Helly-Aa night that the budding expert, in the art of the aff-lay, learnt his job.

The fun and feasting went on till 9 a.m. or later, but in the early sixties, the squads used to foregather about 7 a.m., and, having purloined a large crate, such as is used for the carriage of crockery, would mount it on a sledge or any other contraption to which ropes could be attached. Into the crate were packed as many of the fiddlers as it could hold, and, with the fiddlers fiddling as best they could, it was dragged through the Street. Curiously enough, this custom was confined to Chrismas morning, but it fell into desuetude, and we hear

---

[32]In the olden days, when a country woman made a trip to Lerwick, she would travel as far as the outskirts of the town in her rivlins, and then change into her 'dress' boots which she carried with her in her kishie

no more about it till Christmas, 1886, when an attempt was made to 'revive this ancient custom'. Reference to this revival is made later.

In addition to squad guizing, it was no uncommon thing for one, two or three guizers to 'go out' on their own on any night during the festive season. These 'ploys' were, usually, undertaken on the spur of the moment without previous planning or rehearsal.

Mr Garriock tells us of one occasion on which he had a sudden impulse to carry out a little guizing in his own home. Going up to his father's bedroom, he donned his suit of black clothes. It was many times too large for him, but this was soon overcome by padding it out with pillows and cushions till every button was doing its duty. By way of relieving the funereal look of the suit, he put on a fancy waistcoat which had belonged to an uncle. A suitable mask—there was always a supply of these on hand—and the Sunday 'topper' completed the guizing dress.

Slipping quietly out by the back, he made his way round to the front door, and walked straight into the room where his father sat reading. The aff-lay which followed was anything but complimentary to his father, who, at last, got so exasperated that he ordered him out of the house with a final admonition to the effect that he was the rudest and most impudent guizer it had ever been his misfortune to meet.

Next morning at breakfast, his father, in referring to the incident, said that, if last night's visit was a fair sample, guizing had sadly deteriorated since his young days, and that he could not understand what this younger generation was coming to. The hilarious laughter which followed led to the disclosure that Peter was the culprit. It took him a few moments to realise the situation, and then with a "Well, well, well !" he joined in the laughter against himself. It was a long time, however, before he was allowed to forget that he was incapable of recognising his own Sunday clothes.

Before closing this chapter on guizing, we cannot resist the temptation to recount a very much unrehearsed incident, which befell a guizer who 'gate-crashed' in on another squad.

The hero, or rather the victim, of this incident was a well known young man, whom we shall simply call Jock. An old lady, who remembers this lad well, describes him as a handsome dare-devil young man, who caused many a flutter of the heart-strings among the young ladies of the town. Jock, however, had a somewhat hasty temper which led him into many a scrape, especially when he had a dram. He was, moreover, a great fighter, and, more or less, lorded it over his contemporaries.

The house of the late Provost Leisk was one which was invariably 'open' to the guizers, and was one which had a well merited reputation for 'doing' the guizers well. There had, however, on one occasion, been a free fight in the kitchen between two rival squads, which resulted in Mr Leisk deciding to 'close' his house the following year.

It was one thing to decide to 'close' a popular house, but what is to be done if, in spite of this decision, a squad of guizers marches in and declines to leave? Such was the position when the squad, of which Alick Ratter was a member, marched into Mr Leisk's kitchen next year. In vain did Mr Leisk inform them that the house was 'closed' : the 'boys' insisted that they were not going until they had had a dance. "But what about the lasses?" queried Mr Leask. "We'll get them all right", came the ready reply, and, without waiting to argue the point further, two of the lads went out and, in a very short time, were back with a number of their girl friends. Mr Leisk capitulated and went off to tell his womenfolk to get the 'boys' something to eat and drink.

The kitchen stove was of the American type, and stood

well out into the room. The fire was stoked up and soon the top of the range was red hot and kettles singing, as preparations were made for tea. In view of what happened later, the position of the stove should be borne in mind.

The squad decided that they would have a quadrille, and it so happened that young Ratter and his partner were stationed just in front of the stove. The fiddler struck up a tune, and the dancers had just reached the phase where the 'tops' and 'bottoms' set out on visits to the 'sides', when the door opened, and in wandered Jock. Jock had been celebrating and was in a very bellicose mood. It was now the squad's turn to inform Jock that the house was 'closed', and that this was their 'show', but the more they expostulated, the more was Jock determined to stay, and, just by way of shewing that he meant what he said, he offered to 'take on' the whole damned lot.

The dance came to an abrupt stop, and, rather than create another unfortunate scene, Ratter decided to call Mr Leisk, who, he thought, might have some influence with the intruder. With this in his mind, he crossed the room to where the maid was standing, and asked her to call the master. This was Jock's opportunity as, when Alick turned back to rejoin his partner, he found that his place had been usurped by Jock. This was indeed adding insult to injury, and young Ratter saw red. Striding across the floor, he seized hold of Jock and pushed him away. Jock swayed on his feet, as he squared up to fight, lost his balance, and subsided on the top of the red hot stove.

In his bemused condition, he sat wondering what had pushed him, but before he had time to make up his mind on this point, there was an urge from the rear that sent Jock to his feet with a piercing yell, but not before he had left behind the seat of his breeks and the skin underneath as well. Clasping both hands round the injured portion of his anatomy,

Jock just stood rooted to the spot and cursed and yelled alternately. The lasses screamed and fled; the unsympathetic squad roared with laughter, but even they, at last, took pity on poor Jock's plight. A generous lump of butter was procured from the kitchen cupboard, and was thickly smeared over his injured buttocks. Jock was very sorry for himself as the 'boys' led him gently home.

Jock again appears later in this narrative, but here is another incident in his career which had nothing to do with guizing, and, although it did occur during the Yuletide season, it could scarcely be classified as part of the festivities.

Jock had been having a 'night out' and had attained a jovial, devil-may-care state of mind when he bethought himself that it was time to go home. With erratic steps he made his way along the Street till he came to the foot of the Sooth Kirk Closs (Church Lane), up which he must go before reaching home. Here he halted, pondering whether he could tackle the ascent, then, pulling himself together, he broke into the song "Whaur hae ye bin a' the day, Hielan Laddie, Hielan Laddie?" and lurched up the lane.

He had not gone far before he stumbled against a window and sent his elbow through a pane of glass. The smashing of the glass brought a new idea into Jock's befuddled brain. Lustily continuing his song and staggering up the lane, he punctuated each "Hielan' Laddie" by driving his fist through a window. It was "Whaur hae ye bin a' the day, Hielan' Laddie",—crash—"Hielan' Laddie?"—crash—all the way up.

As each pane of glass was smashed in, out rushed the irate tenants, but such was Jock's reputation as a fighter, that none cared to tackle him in his present mood, so there formed an ever growing procession of raging and fuming householders led by Jock with his "Hielan' Laddie"—crash—"Hielan' Laddie"—crash. By the time the top of the lane had been reached, Jock presented a gruesome spectacle. His hands were torn and bleeding profusely, and his face was smeared and spattered with blood, but he felt nothing and cared less.

In due course he reached the house of friends of his family, and they, seeing his plight, took him in, washed and bound up his hands, then set him down by the fireside and made him drink cups of strong tea. Without a care in the world, Jock fell sound asleep.

The lady of the house went and fetched his father, and he, poor man, was met at the top of Church Lane by an indignant crowd of people all wanting to know who was to pay for the broken panes. To keep the episode quiet, Jock's father—a prominent public official—agreed to send a joiner to repair the damage which turned out to be no less than twentyfive broken panes. Reprehensible, yes, but when viewed through the space of sixty or more years, not without its humour.

CHAPTER XII.

THE OLD ORDER CHANGETH.

MENTION has been made of how after 1874, when the last and greatest Tar-barrel was burned, the authorities definitely prohibited the 'ancient institution', and it looked as if the last of the great Fire Festivals must follow the other two into oblivion, and that future generations would know of them only as 'a tale that is told'.

The Sun-god was not to be so easily thwarted. Throughout the ages, mortals had made obeisance to him, and the tribute, which was his due, must not be withheld simply at the behest of a puny, mundane Town Council. If his annual ascension into his throne in the heavens could not be celebrated in fierce, flaming cauldrons of tar amid shouts and cries of contending factions, then another way must be found, and, sending his edicts forth, into the mind of Youth was born the inspiration—Torches.

Authority, having at last successfully quenched the flames of the Tar-barrel, was in no mood to tolerate any suggestion that they might be rekindled in any form whatsoever, but Youth was not to be denied, and the issue was raised again and again till at last the first torch was lit, and the tribute renewed.

It took two years, however, and many interviews with

the Chief of Police and the Magistrates, before permission
was obtained to have a torchlight procession, and this
permission was only given on the express understanding that
the procession would be in the nature of an experiment, was
not to form a precedent, and that the squads concerned "would
be personally and severally responsible for any damage due to
the burning torches." This injunction did not worry the
'boys' unduly : they had gained their point, but for several
years after the first experiment, the authorities viewed torchlight
processions with genuine alarm.

Old Yule and New'r Day were still considered the
principal days, or rather nights, for the festivities, and it will
be remembered that it was on Yule morning the squads met
about seven o'clock for a grand finale which took the form
of hauling their fiddlers, packed in a crate, through the Street.

It was only natural, therefore, that the first torchlight
procession should be fixed for Yule. It took place at 7 a.m.,
Christmas, 5th January, 1876, and it is recorded that the
procession went from the "North Gate End" to the "South
Gate End", and that "almost all the guizers took part. This
novelty was brought in for the first time this year and seemed
to meet with great approval as a pleasing substitute for other
more tasteless amusements".

The reference to the route of the procession being from
the "North Gate End" to the "South Gate End" is apt to
be puzzling unless one is familiar with the Scots 'gate'—a
road. The word appears in the names of roads such as
Castlegate, Watergate, Trongate or in the expression 'To tak
the gate' (To take to the road). So, in the case of the first
torchlight procession, it is safe to assume that it followed the
old Tar-barrel route from the Gerrison Closs to the Cockstool.
About 150 guizers took part in the procession but less than a
third of that number carried torches.

The *Times* reports that "the usual number of soldiers,

sailors, marines, Turks, Chinamen, Cunningsburghers, male-
ladies and caricatures of local celebrities were to be seen'' but
it would have been interesting had the report given us more
descriptive detail. Why was Cunningsburgh selected to give
its name to a squad? Was there anything peculiar to that
district which differentiated them from the natives of
Scalloway, Sandwick or Delting? And who were the
'male-ladies'? Were they a squad of lads attired in the
fashionable hoop-petticoat who simpered and minced and
flirted or were they prim old maids in flounce and furbelow?
Of one thing we can be sure, it was an ideal dress for guizing
and fun, but we can be equally certain that not even the
slimmest member of the squad could have achieved the
wasp-waist of the period. Then there were the 'local
celebrities'. Were they the fathers of the city or the local
characters of whom there were quite a few? We feel a
grudge against the Editor who, having whetted our interest,
fails to gratify it. He does, however, describe one squad as
''four dark and dropsical looking figures who followed with
cautious steps and slow. The appearance they presented was
that of bottles, fresh from Trent or Burton, and the well-known
label they bore was that of 'Bass' in bright colour and large
size. While gazing upon them and fearful for their safety,
a cynic approached and with bated breath said in our ear
'obliterate the B and you have the proper name of every lover
of *bitter* Bass'. As our new companion had been bitten with
something more powerful than 'Bass', we changed our
standpoint''.

There was no torchlight procession in 1877. We are
not vouchsafed any reason why it was not held, but it is more
than likely that permission was refused because, during the
festive season, a good deal of wanton mischief had been
perpetrated, and, further, the abortive revival of a Tar-barrel
on the previous Up-Helly-Aa had prejudiced the Authorities,

but whatever the reason, it must have been a cogent one as the 'boys' would have been only too keen to repeat the previous year's success.

In the following year, 1878, a torchlight procession was held on the morning of old New'r Day. It is described as a 'novelty' although the same description was applied to the 1876 procession. The novelty was, however, that the torchlight procession preceded the revels, so that this innovation was really a reversion to the Tar-barrel custom. It is interesting to note that, on this occasion, the guizers advertised the procession by sending the bellman round the town. This gave rise to a certain amount of apprehension as the lieges feared that the advertising of the procession was only a dodge to cloak a revival of the Tar-barrel. Their fears proved to be groundless, and the procession was voted "a great success and really a very fine sight".

Torchlight processions were now bidding fair to becoming an established part of the Christmas and New Year festivities, but the Authorities continued to view them with suspicion, and the Specials were kept in readiness to deal with any return to the 'masquerade and saturnalia' of the Tar-barrel. That they were justified is borne out by the fact, already narrated, that it was this year which saw the last attempt at its revival.

The guizers, who were mainly responsible for organising the torchlight processions, were now beginning to assume authority, and in the following year we are introduced to the precursor of the Bill. On the day before New'r Day (old style), there was affixed to the Market Cross a placard which intimated that a "Torchlight procession would be formed by the guizers before commencing their visitations".

The torches were lit at 2.30 a.m., and the route taken was from the Market Cross northwards, round the Hillhead and back to the Market Cross, "where the torches were extinguished and the sticks stacked with great regularity and precision''. No doubt, the careful stacking of the sticks was done under the eyes of the police, and had been part of the bargain before permission was granted to hold the procession. From the meagre reports available, this procession must have been a very straggling one, but towards the finish, when ''all the fiddlers had got into better trim, it had a very striking effect''. We are not told whether the fiddlers were massed as a band or whether each one headed his own squad, but the straggling of the squads would indicate that the latter is more probable.

We now come to a very important change in the festivities. For some years back, public opinion had been veering round to the view that the festivities should be held in accordance with the 'new style' calendar. The first attempt to do this was tried out on Christmas Day, 1879, and New Year's Day, 1880. The majority of the public approved of the change but a good many of the younger folk were determined to retain the 'old style'. Perhaps they saw the chance of duplicating their nights of frivolities ! A number of youths did, in fact, attempt to continue the celebrations on the old dates, and the Editor of the *Times* has to remind them that ''most people would consider that to stay up all night once a week would be rather over-doing it . . . . We would remind them that going about in disguise, is a punishable offence under the Police Act, and that it is only by the tolerance of the magistrates that it is allowed''. He further warns them that ''pistol firing, if detected, may lead to prosecution and a fine for a breach of the Gun Licence Act''.

With the change of the dates, another matter was brought to the forefront. The older folks, on whom lay the task of keeping open house and giving entertainment, were feeling the strain of waiting up for the guizers. In the Tar-barrelling days, the fun really commenced at midnight, and from then onwards there was always plenty of excitement to keep everyone

awake, but now there was nothing to do before the first of the
squads put in an appearance about 3 a.m. Hosts and hostesses,
to say nothing of their guests, grew weary of waiting up or,
as some did, going to bed and then getting up again before
the guizers arrived. Some houses which had always been
'open' ceased to entertain and others had let it be known that
they, too, would 'close'.

The hosts and hostesses met, talked matters over and
decided to intimate to the guizers that it was their wish that
the festivities should commence in the evening. The guizers
opposed this innovation and "threats were freely indulged in
of dire vengeance against any who might attempt to come out
during the evening . . . . Much negotiation took place as if
the subject had been the Treaty of Berlin". A compromise
was, eventually, reached, and it was publicly announced that
guizing would commence at 1 a.m. on Christmas morning with
a torchlight procession. The Weather Clerk, however, had
his views, too, about this innovation, for he ordained a storm,
and the bellman had to be sent round announcing the
postponement of the procession till the same hour on New
Year's morning. The weather might damp the procession but
it did not interfere with the guizing which was carried on as
usual.

Christmas Day, 1879, is also memorable in the history
of Lerwick's gay season. It is recorded that "in the evening
a most unusual attraction in Lerwick was the theatre in
Mounthooly Street Hall, where Siddons' company played
'Rob Roy' to a crowded house". Mounthooly Street Hall
was originally a Wesleyan chapel which was converted into a
public hall. It stood on the site now occupied by the Rechabite
Hall.

The postponed procession took place on New Year's
morning, and made a "very attractive sight" but it was not
carried through without incident. Previous processions had

been rather haphazard, go-as-you-please affairs. On this occasion, it was decided that Alick Ratter and Peter W. Greig would act as marshals and direct the proceedings. Our old friend Jock was also there with his squad.

The muster took place at the Market Cross, and torches had been handed out. The marshals had decided that the procession should go 'nort' alang' but Jock, whose squad was at the tail end, decided that it should go 'sooth alang'. The newly appointed marshals were worried : the procession was ready to start but they dared not give the signal to light up until they were sure that, on the order to march, it would not break in two and proceed in opposite directions. The head end was shouting "Nort' alang" and the tail end was just as vociferously yelling "Sooth alang". An *impasse* had been reached and the guizers were beginning to get out of hand when Ratter appealed to Greig to go back and try to persuade Jock to fall in with the pre-arranged order of route. Greig was not hopeful but said he would try, and set off to interview Jock. The interview, so far as Peter was concerned, was not successful, and in a few minutes he was returning with his hands covering his face and the blood streaming copiously from his nose. "What's wrong?" asked Alick. Raising his hands for a moment from a gory face, Peter looked up and replied, "He hit me". Jock had given his answer ; the argument was finished : the procession went 'sooth alang !'. It says much for the gameness of Peter that he not only continued to assist Alick to marshal the procession but actually took his full share in the guizing and dancing afterwards. His nose and face were so badly swollen that, more than once during the morning, he was informed that he could quite easily dispense with his mask.

This incident led to the suggestion that there should be an 'appointed captain or marshal', but two years more had to elapse before this suggestion was put into effect.

So far, torchlight processions had taken place only at Christmas or New Year, and this conformed to the regular squad guizing nights. Up-Helly-Aa was still the 'free lance' night when individuals or nondescript squads made merry. In 1881, however, a break was made with long established custom. In this year, the torchlight procession took place on Up-Helly-Aa, and was marked by the first signs of real organisation. The procession of sixty torches started from the Market Cross, marched to the south end of the town, then countermarched and made its way back to the north end. At this point it wheeled and returned to the Cross where the torches were extinguished. It is described as being "singularly brilliant and the largest turn-out of its kind that has ever taken place".

On this occasion, too, the wishes of the hosts prevailed : the procession started at nine o'clock and, as soon as it was over, the guizers carried out their usual round of visits.

Old customs die hard, and the following Christmas and New Year saw a return to the 2 a.m. start. There were many complaints from hosts and hostesses, and more houses shut their doors. 'There are none so blind as those that will not see' runs the proverb, and, by their lack of consideration for those who opened their houses and entertained them, the guizers were slowly but surely killing the 'ancient customs' on which they put so much store.

CHAPTER XIII.

THE year 1882 is a red-letter year in the annals of Lerwick. His Royal Highness the Duke of Edinburgh, as Admiral Superintendent of Naval Reserves, was on a tour of duty inspecting Coast Guards and Royal Naval Reserves. He was due to arrive in Lerwick on 24th January, and had graciously consented to lay the foundation stone of the new Town Hall.

The town was all agog with excitement, and most elaborate efforts were made to make the Duke's visit a right royal one. Flags and bunting fluttered from innumerable flagstaffs, windows and railings while, at night, the town was illuminated with coloured lights and lanterns till, as one contemporary has expressed it, the whole place looked like fairyland.

As the visit coincided with the last days of the festivities, the guizers were keen that the Duke should have the opportunity of witnessing the Up-Helly-Aa celebrations, and for this purpose they decided to put the date forward to the twentyfourth in place of the statutory twentyninth.

Sometime earlier the guizers had met to appoint a Captain or Marshal. While all were convinced that such an official was very necessary, they could not agree over his

G

nomenclature. Both 'Captain' and 'Marshal' were considered much too prosaic. In the discussion which followed the proposal of these titles, the meeting almost forgot the purpose for which it had met till someone, more as a joke than anything else, suggested that 'Worthy Chief Guizer' might solve the difficulty. This title met with the approval of the majority, and Peter W. Greig, later one of the partners and editors of the *Shetland Times*, was duly elected the first Worthy Chief Guizer.

The public committee in charge of the celebrations and entertainments in connection with the Duke's visit had approached the guizers and asked them to organise a torchlight procession. This request was readily granted, and the guizers promised that they would turn out with between 90 and 100 torches.

The *Times* records :—"We are informed by the Worthy Chief Guizer that, on the night of the illumination, guizers are to assemble at North Hillhead, where torches will be lighted up at 9 o'clock. We trust the night will be fine, and a good display made. We would, however, take the opportunity of impressing upon our young friends the necessity of being very careful, as any damage arising from the torches would be extremely regrettable". Another extract proclaims that "each torchbearer will be dressed in a fantastic garb, and, if the Duke should condescend to look on the scene, we fancy he will think it most unique".

The Editor of the *Times* was not the only one who viewed the prospects of a torchlight procession with some alarm. Mr Ratter related how, when at work in the *Times* office, the sheriff officer called and handed to him a letter from Sheriff Rampini which stated that it had come to the notice of his Lordship that he, Alexander Ratter, was organising a torchlight procession for the night of the twentyfourth January, and that, in the event of such a procession taking place and any damage resulting therefrom, he, Alexander Ratter, would be held liable for any such damage.

This was a blow, and young Ratter immediately decided that, so far as he was concerned, he would have nothing to do with the procession. He showed the letter to his friend, Peter Greig, who also read it with dismay. "Why shöd da Sheriff fix upo' me?" asked Alick. "Du is da Worthy Chief Guizer, an' du his as muckle ta dae wi' hit as me". "Yea, Boy, I ken dat. I tink du hid better see R.B." 'R.B.' was the late R. B. Hunter, at that time an apprentice in the Union Bank, and one of the stalwarts among the guizers. To R.B. went Ratter, and he advised him to see Mr John Leisk (later Provost of Lerwick), one of the promoters of the celebrations. Ratter called on him, and handed over the letter. Mr Leisk read it through, pondered over the contents for a few moments, and a smile gradually spread over his face. Dropping into the vernacular, he addressed Ratter. "Alick, haes du ony money?" "No Maister Leisk, I cudna' say dat I hiv". "Heh, heh! I tocht dat: du hisna' a penny. Du needna' worry aboot damages. Go du ahead. Damages! Ha, hah! Damages! Ha, ha, hah!"

Alick returned in high glee to his chums, and reported the result of his interview with Mr Leisk. As each of the 'boys' was, more or less, in the same precarious financial position as Alick, the Sheriff's letter was 'allowed to lie on the table', and preparations were pushed forward to make the procession worthy of the occasion. Instead now of the tardy and 'liable for damages' permission from the authorities, the guizers were actually being encouraged to do their best by a committee of leading citizens. Later, it also transpired that among those who were most enthusiastic about the torchlight procession, was the Sheriff himself, but like many another in authority, he had to place his official duty before his own private desires. Sheriff Rampini was a popular and much respected judge, so when it became known that his sympathies were with the guizers, all fear of the law disappeared, and they made it a point of honour that they would not let him down.

When one remembers that the greatest number of torches, mustered in previous processions, was about sixty, it says much for the enthusiasm of the newly appointed Worthy Chief Guizer and his henchmen that, 'on the night of the illumination', they paraded with one hundred and thirty.

The original intention of starting from the North Hillhead was departed from, and the guizers assembled at the more usual starting place, the Market Cross. Special efforts were made to make the costumes as fantastic and varied as possible but, unfortunately, we are not told what they represented nor are they even described. The torches were lit at 9 p.m. and the procession marched through Commercial Street, wound its way over the narrow road below Fort Charlotte and entered the Fort through the north gate. Once inside, the guizers marched round the parade ground till they had formed a large circle, then, raising their torches high above their heads, they gave three cheers for the Duke. Forming into line again they left the Fort by the west gate, and made their way past the new Town Hall.

It was at this point that young Ratter had cause to remember the Sheriff's warning. The building was encased in scaffolding, and, as befitted the occasion of the laying of the foundation stone, from every spar and pole flew long strings of bunting. A strong westerly breeze was blowing, and, as the procession passed, one of the torches came in contact with a string of flags. In less time than it takes to tell, the flames shot up the string, other strings became involved, and for a moment or two, as the burning flags twisted and fluttered round the timber, it looked as if the scaffolding was on fire. It was an anxious moment, but beyond adding an unrehearsed item to the fireworks displays, no material damage was done, and the procession carried on along the Hillhead.

The route now took the procession past the Sheriff's residence. Here a halt was made and, by way of shewing their appreciation of his attitude—unofficial—towards the guizers, they gave him three resounding cheers. They then made their way down Mounthooly Street, marched to the south end of Commercial Street and returned to the Cross.

The finish of this procession was marked by an event which foreshadowed the elaborate bonfires of later days. At the finish of all previous torchlight processions, the torches had to be extinguished and "the sticks stacked with great regularity and precision". On this occasion, the sticks were piled up to make a great bonfire "which fascinated the immense crowd of sightseers". When we think of the blaze of modern days, we may be allowed a quiet smile at the great bonfire of one hundred and thirty sticks. Still, everything has to have a beginning, and little did the guizers of 1882 think of the effect their bonfire would have in the years which lay ahead.

After the bonfire, the guizing squads, each headed by its own fiddler, carried out the usual round of visitations.

History does not relate whether "the Duke condescended to look upon the scene" or whether he thought it "most unique" but it is recorded that the procession was carried through with "the most thorough discipline" and that "the worthy Superintendent of Police was never called upon to say a cross word the whole evening".

So ended the 24th January, 1882, a day which, for many a year, was to remain vivid in the memories of all who were privileged to feast and entertain the royal Duke of Edinburgh.

In relating the activities of the guizers on this historic occasion, no reference has been made to the many other forms of entertainment provided for welcoming His Royal Highness,

but these do not come strictly within the purview of this
narrative.   Suffice it to say that from all parts of the county,
by boat, on pony and on foot, high and low flocked to the
Capital to join with the citizens in fêting, feasting and
entertaining him on a scale which has never, before or since,
been equalled in Shetland.

CHAPTER XIV.

THE DOLDRUMS.

THE efforts put forth on the occasion of the Duke of Edinburgh's visit would seem to have exhausted the fervour of the guizers. For the next year or two, a sort of apathy spread over the twentyfour days of Yule. To what cause can we ascribe this state of affairs? One might say that the weather had something to do with it. On the following Christmas and Up-Helly-Aa it was very bad, but on New Year's Day it was ideal. Much the same conditions prevailed the next year, but weather conditions and muddy streets had never before damped the enthusiasm of the guizers. It would be untrue to say that there were no guizers abroad : there was, indeed, quite a number, but the celebrations are described as being very lifeless and, moreover, there were very few houses 'open'.

"Very few houses 'open' "—there seems little doubt that this was the real cause for the decline of guizing during this period. Householders simply would not wait up till the early hours of the morning for the reception of the squads, and the *Times* is moved to predict "that unless some radical change is made with regard to the time it is indulged in, guizing will soon become a custom more honoured in the breach than in the observance".

Even First Footing on New Year's morning, which had
been growing in favour in recent years, was scarcely indulged
in.

This lull in the usual liveliness of the festive season was
probably directly responsible for an innovation at New Year.
The demonstrations are described as most unusual. As the
town clock ushered in 1883, "several bells in the town and on
board the vessels in the harbour were merrily rung, while a
large crowd, which had assembled at the Old Tolbooth, set up
a deafening cheer, and the 'tooing' of 'looder-horns' was
heard in all directions. Coloured lights blazed from various
parts of the town, and from the *St. Clair*, which was lying in
the harbour, some beautiful rockets were set off".

It was no innovation to usher in the New Year with
crackers and locder-horns : that had been customary beyond
the memory of the oldest inhabitant; but bell-ringing was a
new development, and the coloured lights which blazed
throughout the town must surely have been surplus stores left
over from the Duke's visit.

Up-Helly-Aa, 1883, registered the depth of the
depression, for there was not a single house 'open', and people
were asking where this time-honoured institution was drifting
to? Some, indeed, were rejoicing that it would soon bring
itself to a well-deserved termination. Such guizers as did
turn out "were a lot of young fellows capering about in
disguises, mostly of a rude and ridiculous character. As there
were no people silly enough to open their houses, the maskers
had to content themselves with making noises and committing
small acts of mischief along the streets". Truly, guizing had
fallen on evil times.

The following Christmas and New Year did not shew
much improvement : fewer guizers were abroad, and their
dresses were poor. So sure was the *Times* that guizing was
doomed, that it facetiously suggests that "before the last

flicker of the fire goes out, it might be advisable that local antiquarians should secure a specimen of a 'guizer' before that worthy is entirely extinct, have him stuffed and deposited in some safe corner as the last remnant of an old custom, and the first contribution towards a new Museum for Lerwick''.

This year, too, we hear for the first time of the '' 'peerie guizers' who go a-hunting on Christmas Eve, and that so far as they are concerned the juveniles shewed unmistakably that the custom is not decaying with them. Their aim is generally acknowledged to be a mercenary one''. Although the peerie guizers are brought to our notice for the first time, they had been an integral part of the Christmas celebrations for many years.

The year 1883 had, at least, one triumph. It will be remembered that, in 1879, Lerwick adopted the new style dates for Christmas and New Year. In this, Lerwick had been severely left to its new-fangled notions. Even its neighbour, Bressay, across the harbour, would have none of it, and "looked with pity on the Lerwegians, who have so ruthlessly cast aside the customs of their forefathers''. The hamlet of Sound, however, which boasts in the couplet that "Soond was Soond when Lerwick was nane, and Soond will be Soond when Lerwick is gane'', fell into line with the Capital, and "showed to the world that it has advanced to a stage at which antiquated custom will receive no countenance''.

Many years were to pass before the 'new style' dates began to be adopted in the country, and, even in this year of 1946, there are still quite a number of districts which tenaciously cling to the 'old style' Yule and New'r Day, and it is only a year or two since Bressay ceased to "look with pity on Lerwegians who had so ruthlessly cast aside the customs of their forefathers''.

New Year, 1884, received a poor welcome in comparison with 1883. The Free Kirk bell tolled the old year out, and a salvo of small and big guns welcomed the new year in. There was a decline in the number of guizers, and those who did venture forth wore dresses which ''had been good at one time''—a rather scathing comment. In this year, too, there was a considerable amount of rowdyism and wanton damage to property, and the Specials had to be posted at ''points of advantage''. Each constable was armed with a nine-inch club which had been specially made by order of the magistrates.

The more orderly section of the guizers realised that unless something were done to put a stop to the disreputable behaviour which had characterised the past few years, guizing would be prohibited all together, and efforts were made to put it on a more law-abiding basis. New Year's day, 1885, saw a marked improvement in the behaviour of the guizers, and, although there was another outbreak of gas-lamp and window smashing, the rowdyism was fortunately confined to a very few individuals.

In passing it is of interest to record, that on New Year's Day, the Lerwick Brass Band, numbering twelve instruments, made its first appearance in public at the head of the annual Royal Naval Reserve procession.

Encouraged by the improvement on New Year's Day, the Worthy Chief Guizer and his committee were now determined to rehabilitate the guizers in the eyes of the public, and, by way of asserting control, organised a torchlight procession for nine o'clock on the evening of Up-Helly-Aa. In this they were very successful, being able to muster about eighty torches, and to effect a great improvement in the dresses. It was most unfortunate that on Up-Helly-Aa night the weather was very bad. The rain came down in torrents and the roads were a sea of mud. This spoilt what might have been a very successful night, and the festivities were of short duration.

From now onwards, the Worthy Chief Guizer and his

committee began to exercise more control, and, as their authority became recognised and respected, so did acts of hooliganism by the guizers decline.

It was about this time, too, that a gradual change was coming over time-honoured custom. Fewer organised squads were going out at Christmas and New Year, and such squads as did go out on these nights, were not dressed in uniform costumes; but the real cause of the decline of Christmas and New Year guizing was, undoubtedly, the fact that the squads would persist in starting their visitations at 2 a.m. and later, with the inevitable result that they found fewer and fewer houses 'open'.

Up-Helly-Aa was coming rapidly to the forefront as the principal night of the festivities, and, as a new phase in guizing was being inaugurated, we can close this chapter in its history without regret.

CHAPTER XV.

THE first fruits of the new administration was the elimination of unruly elements at Up-Helly-Aa. No attempt was made to exercise supervision at Christmas or New Year, and the Specials continued to be posted on these nights at 'points of advantage' to deal with attempts at wanton mischief.

The Worthy Chief Guizer and his committee took full charge of all the arrangements for the 1886 Up-Helly-Aa celebrations. For the first time we hear of a Torch Committee but no indication is given as to what their duties were. Were they the actual makers of the torches or did they simply see that sufficient were forthcoming and superintend their distribution? We are not told but we do know that, prior to 1882, each squad taking part in a procession, made its own torches. Another innovation was made : two men were engaged to look after the torches, soak them in paraffin, and hand them over to the guizers as they went to take their places in the procession.

On the day before Up-Helly-Aa large placards were posted throughout the town intimating that "All Guizers intending to take part in the procession will assemble at the Market Cross at 8.30 on Friday evening". At this hour a red flare was lit on the top of the Cross as a signal for the guizers to muster, and, thereafter, the squads began to assemble, each with a fiddler at its head. The marshals then took charge; the procession was formed up; the Worthy Chief Guizer gave the order to light up, and, at precisely nine o'clock, the procession moved off. Order had been established.

This procession finished up at the north end of the Esplanade "where a large heap of combustibles had been gathered and the torch sticks were heaped on the top of it". The guizers gathered round the bonfire, and a piper struck up a lively tune. "The guizers danced round the blazing pile 'in wild and savage glee' ".

So far, everything had gone off splendidly, but afterwards, the guizers suffered a bitter disappointment—very few houses were 'open' to receive them. It may be that the weather, which was stormy, had some effect in producing this state of matters, but, in the main, it was the result of the decadence of guizing in the previous few years. The fault did not lie with the new organisation but rather in the fact that would-be hosts had been disappointed or, to put it in the more expressive slang of modern days, 'fed up' with the want of consideration on the part of the guizers for their hosts, and the rejection of their repeated appeals for an earlier start in the visitations.

Up-Helly Aa 1886 is notable for a feature which was the prototype of many such in years to come. Guizers were beginning to look out for new ideas, and it was only natural that they turned to topical events for inspiration. A distinct break-away from custom was made when one squad staged a pantomimic show instead of depicting a number of uniformly dressed characters.

Marching along in the middle of the procession went an old country woman, dressed in homespuns, hap, thick woollen

stockings and rivlins. Under her left arm she carried a large
sheaf of corn, while in her right hand she held the end of
a 'tedder' at the other end of which strained a rather
recalcitrant cow whose buttings, bellows and antics indicated
that it was no ordinary 'coo'. It was, in fact, the complete
hide of a cow—horns, hooves, tail and all—which was
stretched over a shaped framework, inside which a guizer
manipulated its charges into the crowd, and its kicking and
rearing. Behind stumped the 'old man', in woollen jersey,
tattered coat and breeks, the extremities of which were tucked
into his hose, while on his head was an old Yaki (Greenland)
furry cap. With a stout stick, he belaboured the hind quarters
of the cow, and adjured her to take no notice 'o' dis toon
trash'. The true significance of the topical theme which this
squad portrayed was only apparent after the squad had passed :
on the back of the 'old man' was affixed a placard bearing
the then famous Gladstonian slogan—"Three Acres and a
Coo".

Along the Street they went, undaunted by the
unaccustomed throng. From all sides pertinent, but mostly
impertinent questions were flung, and just as pertinently
answered. The cow, being debarred from human speech,
marked her approval or disapproval according to the sentiment
of the remarks, ribald or otherwise.

It was this year, too, which saw the first juvenile
Up-Helly-Aa torchlight procession. At about 7.30 in the
evening, a dozen or more youngsters in guizing dress 'lit up' a
few torches and marched round the town. That these
youngsters were allowed to march through the town with
lighted torches is, indeed, proof that, at long last, the fears
and suspicions of those in authority had been allayed, and
that torches had become one of the chief attractions of the
festivities.

The "Committee of Management", by which name the

Worthy Chief Guizer and his lieutenants were now known, was very disheartened by the lack of 'open' houses, and determined, before another Up-Helly-Aa came round, that they must regain the goodwill of the hosts and hostesses. On 7th December, 1886, we have a record of the first Guizers' Meeting. Somewhere over seventy guizers met in the 'Auld Kirk' which stood on the site now occupied by the Free Masons' Hall, and which, at that time, served the purpose of a public hall.

The meeting had been called for the express purpose of fixing an earlier hour for the commencement of house visitations, "otherwise", as one orator declared, "within a few years at the most, however much we may regret it, guizing will be a thing of the past". The hour suggested was nine or ten o'clock, and, after a very considerable amount of discussion and oratory, the latter hour was agreed upon.

It sounds strange to our ears to hear that one of the chief difficulties in arranging for an early starting hour was, that the lads in the shops could not get off in time to allow them to join in the revels. A committee was appointed to interview the merchants, and to request them to allow any of their assistants, who wished to take part in the guizing, to get off work at 9.30. The 'Shop Assistants Act' had not even been dreamt of in those days, and it was no uncommon thing for merchants to keep their shops open all night at Christmas and New Year.

One has to remember that, although Up-Helly-Aa with its torchlight procession was rapidly becoming the chief night of the revels, Christmas and New Year were still thought of as the proper guizing nights, and one of the main purposes of the meeting was to encourage a revival of guizing on these nights. That the meeting's recommendations were acted on, at least for the time being, is borne out by the fact that there was a large turn-out of guizers on Christmas Eve, and that a great number of houses were 'open'.

On Christmas Eve, too, great excitement was caused by an announcement that a squad was to revive the 'ancient custom' of dragging a crate through the Street. It proved to be a poor imitation, and was not well received. The *Times* reported that "about 10.30 the squad with the 'crate' came upon the scene. The crate was done up with a green canopy and gaily decorated with holly, while Chinese lanterns were suspended from the roof. Inside was seated the 'Old Professor' with the fiddle, 'Jeems' himself being decorated with an ancient tile of the chimney-pot persuasion. The squad—numbering eight—were very gaily dressed. The crate to all appearance was a great disappointment to the public, as it looked exceedingly small when on the street, and not very attractive''.

It is quite evident that this revival was purely a squad affair, and one single fiddler—no matter how well dressed— in a small crate, to say nothing of a gaily decorated green canopy with Chinese lanterns and holly, could have very little in common with a crateful of fiddlers bouncing along at the end of a rope on Christmas morning.

There is no doubt that the special efforts of the Committee of Management did, for a time, help to preserve the old regular guizing nights, but, as time went on, Christmas and New Year guizing, as organised festivities, declined, and in the Nineties practically disappeared. Christmas Eve, although by no means neglected by adults, came to be recognised as the night for the 'peerie guizers', while New Year's Eve became the prerogative of the First Fitters who gradually discarded the squad dress, and adopted the nondescript or 'family group' style of guizing which was, formerly, practised only on Up-Helly-Aa.

In scanning the reports of Up-Helly-Aa from this period

onwards, we find that each successive festival is described as 'the finest', 'the greatest', 'the most outstanding', 'unparalleled' and so on. If the facts about the progressive improvements made each year were not known, these repeated superlatives might be put down as journalese. This, however, is not the case, as, with a few exceptions, each succeeding Up-Helly-Aa tended to outshine the previous one in organisation and brilliance.

In spite of very disagreeable weather, Up-Helly-Aa 1887 was a great success. The torchlight procession "was the most successful ever held". It was headed by a piper, and 'mustered' over a hundred torches. Probably on account of the weather, the route of the procession was confined to north along Commercial Street, back by the Esplanade to the Market Cross, thence to the South End, back to the North End and back again to Victoria Pier "where torch sticks and other combustibles were converted into a huge bonfire". The report continues, "The thanks of all are due to the 'Committee of Management' who exerted themselves to procure the torches . . . while thanks are also due to those gentlemen who kindly responded to the calls on them, and subscribed towards the fund".

Although this was the first occasion on which there is any reference to a collection having been made to defray the cost of the torches, collections had been made for most, if not all, previous processions, and it is only a few years ago since one of the earliest books—a halfpenny passbook—was destroyed during a spring-cleaning. It showed a total of under Three Pounds subscribed by various merchants, and the disbursements covered the cost of sticks and paraffin for about 100 torches and a gratuity to Harry Stephen, plumber, for giving them a final dip before being handed out to the guizers. There is no mention of any expenditure for sacking. Enough said !

H

The year 1888 brought the Brass Band into prominence. On New Year's Eve it marched to the Market Cross, and for the first time played the Old Year out and the New Year in; thereafter, "it executed a number of airs in fine style at the junction of Hillhead and Scalloway Road, which was highly appreciated by the people". On the two previous New Year's Days, it had led the Royal Naval Reserve on their annual processions through the town, but on this New Year's Day "it does seem strange that a force of five or six hundred men cannot, or will not subscribe among themselves the trifle necessary to pay the Band". This reproof had the desired effect, and on subsequent R.N.R. processions the Band again led the way.

So far, previous torchlight processions had had to be content with the services of a piper to lead the way, but, now, the Committee of Management decided that nothing less than the Brass Band would grace the head of the procession, and, undeterred by 'the trifle necessary' to pay for its services, they engaged it for Up-Helly-Aa. The Committee also issued an order that none but guizers would be allowed to take part in the procession.

The procession itself, was a well organised one of roughly one hundred torchbearers : the Band led the way, "while the Worthy Chief occupied the van, armed with a larger torch than any of the rest". On its return to the Market Cross, the Band played several lively tunes while the bonfire merrily burned. Afterwards, the Band received a hearty vote of thanks for their services, and hopes were expressed "when another year comes round, the Band will again contribute their musical abilities to the procession".

CHAPTER XVI.

GALLEYS.

ONE does not associate the name 'Galley' with a Viking Long-ship : its very sound conjures up visions of sweating slaves driving the Roman triremes across the Mediterranean Sea or Barbary pirates lying in wait for their prey, and yet, 'Galley' was the name the guizers bestowed on the Viking Long-ships which they introduced into their Up-Helly-Aa processions.

The young men, who organised the processions, would not have troubled their heads about the precise nomenclature of Viking fighting ships. The captain's galley from a visiting Man-o'-war or a Greenland whaler was a familiar sight in Lerwick harbour, but whether or not this suggested the name, they called their festival ship a 'Galley'. Even when, in later years, the Docks Boys made models of modern battleships or whaling steamers, these were also called the Docks Boys' Galleys, so as 'Galleys' they first made their appearance at Up-Helly-Aa, and 'Galleys' they are likely to remain.

The Worthy Chief Guizer and the Committee of Management were now really getting into their stride. They had overcome the apathy of many of the householders about opening their houses for the entertainment of the guizers, and had established authority over all those who wished to join

in the processions.   Their next effort towards the improvement
of the celebrations was a momentous one.   It was in 1889 that
the Long-ship or Norse Galley, as it was called, made its first
appearance in a torchlight procession.   The author of this
innovation is not recorded but, in all probability, it was the
young talented author and poet, J. J. Haldane Burgess.   He
was steeped in Norse lore, and, in later years, was the
recognised consultant to the Up-Helly-Aa Committee on all
matters appertaining to Norse Long-ships, heraldic designs and
costumes of the Vikings.   Up till this year there are no
indications that the torchlight procession signified anything
more than a good substitute for the prohibited Tar-barrel and
an excellent start-off to the Up-Helly-Aa celebrations.   Now,
the blazing torches began to be considered the counterpart of
the old Nordic sacrificial fires, and still further symbolism was
added by the introduction of the Long-ship which, bearing
the body of the Viking Jarl, was sent on its voyage to Valhalla
in a blaze of fire.

On Up-Helly-Aa, about one hundred and twenty guizers
assembled at the Market Cross at 9 p.m., and, after having
been marshalled and supplied with torches, they marched and
countermarched round the Cross and then ''headed north along
Commercial Street, followed by the 'war galley'—an erection
on wheels, built after the style of the heraldic 'Dragon Ship'
with high stem and stern''.

On board the Galley were two fiddlers, Archie Robb and
Robbie Paton, who could be seen 'laying at da fiddle', but
the tumultuous cheering which greeted the Galley completely
drowned their efforts so that their music had to be taken on
trust.

The first Up-Helly-Aa Galley did not have a smooth
passage.   A gale had sprung up which forced the Galley's
crew to 'andoo'[33] in sheltered havens while the procession

---

[33]Andoo:—Pulling on the oars of a boat just sufficient to stem the
tide.   As used in the text—Heave-to.

Up-Helly-Aa Torchlight Procession.

A. E. DOROTHY JOHNSON, D.A.

CHIEF CONSTABLE MACKAY.

TYPE OF UPHELLY A' GALLEY. 12 FT LONG, USED FROM 1895 to 1907.

THE GALLEY ENLARGED TO 16 FEET UPHELLY-A' 1908.

EARLY UP-HELLY-AA GALLEYS

A MODERN UP-HELLY-AA GALLEY.

THE END OF THE VOYAGE.
(Procession encircling the galley before throwing in the torches.)

THE BILL, 1939.

GUIZER JARL, 1925.
(He is here wearing the first Jarl's dress.
The latest dress and accoutrements are described on page 157.)

PANSHINE MARY'S BODYGUARD, 1933.

DISMAL DESMOND, 1937.

GUIZER JARL AND HIS VIKINGS, 1921.

GUIZER JARL AND HIS SQUAD (Erik the Red), 1939.

SCOTTISH ARCHERS, 1939.

DA CAIRDIN', 1939.
(The carding of the wool was always an excuse for a social evening in Shetland.)

SAVOYARDS, 1938.

GUIZER JARL AND SQUAD (Hjaltlanders), 1938.

SKEKLERS, 1939.
(See foot of page 79.)

NIGHT BIRDS, 1936.

JOHN PEEL, 1936.

OI ! (The Lambeth Walk), 1939.

wended its way over the usual route. It was taken to the south end of Commercial Street to await the return of the procession. When the procession did return, the Galley was no longer relegated to the tail end but proudly took the lead "in fine style, little knowing, like many a noble ship, that her end was so near; for, as soon as a halt was made at the Cross, the blazing torches were tossed into her, and soon her goodly proportions with their painted and gilded ornaments were wrapt in a sheet of flame".

The good ship, however, was not allowed to end her career without one more voyage. The old Tar-barrel spirit was not yet quite dead, for no sooner had the Galley received her last freight of burning torches, than there was a rush to man the drag-ropes, and, before the Committee could interefere, she was careering north along the Esplanade. Arriving at Burns Rails, which railed off the roadway now bounded by the North of Scotland Bank and the Scottish Co-operative Society's premises, the Galley was swung into Commercial Street, and raced back to the Cross where it collapsed and became a glorious bonfire which was finally extinguished by the Specials. It was a well conceived plot by a number of guizers, and must have warmed the heart of every old Tar-barreller present.

In the following year, 1890, the Committee issued its first illuminated Collecting Sheet, which is described as "most ferociously artistic" and "enough to draw money from a stone". It would have been of interest to have had the full text of this appeal, but from the scraps vouchsafed to us, the first illuminated collecting sheet was not unlike those of the present day. It opened with the "determination of the Guizers of Lerwick to revere their forefathers and reflect credit on themselves", and finished with "We are too proud to work, too chicken-hearted to steal, but we have this little LIST to which we hope you will add''.

The 1890 procession was, more or less, a repetition of that of the previous year. There was a gaily decorated Norse Galley which headed the procession, and anchored for the last time at the head of Victoria pier. The Committee and the Specials prevented further unauthorised cruises.

On Christmas Eve of that year, it is worth noting that one squad went out representing all the characters in the then very popular *Uncle Tom's Cabin*, and this new departure so caught the public fancy, it was suggested that it was well worthy of imitation.

Up-Helly-Aa 1891 was, for some unknown reason, held one week later than customary. A large placard, posted on the Market Cross, intimated that the ceremony would be held on the 5th February with a grand torchlight procession, and the notice was signed by the Worthy Chief Guizer, and sealed with his mark—an impression of a human foot.

The festival was preceded by an 'assessment' on the merchants and professional gentlemen in the town. The full contents of this Collecting Sheet are on record, and were as follows :—

UP-HELLY-AA.

To the most Honourable Inhabitants of the
Ancient Burgh of Lerwick, the prayer of the Worthy
Guizers of the said Burgh HUMBLY SHEWETH :

1.—That it is our desire to celebrate the ancient festival of "Up-Helly-Aa" with a Grand Torchlight Procession.

2.—That not being blessed with a surfeit of that commodity variously known as Filthy Lucre, The Root of all Evil, or the more vulgar terms of Brass, Tin or Maikes, we must apply to the foresaid Honourables for help to raise the needful.

GENTLEMEN—No sum will be too large. With a light heart throw something heavy into the hat, and with a lighter heart and a lighter flame we will send its ashes to join the ashes of our venerable forefathers.

And your Petitioners will ever Pray—

Donors of £1 will be presented with a brand new "Sunlight" advertising tablet for affixing to the doors of their domiciles. Donors of £5 will receive an award of merit signed by the W.C.G., and donors of £10 will have their sanity enquired into by the Authorities.

The procession led by the now indispensable Town Band, and headed by an ancient Norse Galley gaily decorated with flags and manned by a number of gaudily attired fiddlers, was a great success. There were over one hundred torchbearers in dresses which were colourful and attractive.

Variety was given to this procession by the inclusion of an old-time 'crate' which brought up the rear. This 'crate' seems to have been, more or less, a copy of the one which so disappointed old guizers on Christmas morning, 1887. It was very prettily decorated with a canopy of pink curtains, and illuminated with Chinese lanterns while inside two fiddlers plied their bows with might and main.

Another touch of variety was given by a lone guizer who masqueraded in the now almost obsolete 'gloy'[34] dress. This was the old straw guizing dress of the Skudler which has already been described in a previous chapter. It attracted a great deal of interest and came in for special mention in the Press.

---

[34]Gloy :—Straight, clean, unbroken straw as used for making kishies, flakkies, etc. *See* Note 24.

The guizers of Up-Helly-Aa, 1891, seem to have been imbued, more than usual, with memories of the past. Great excitement and amusement were caused by the appearance of a Tar-barrel but it had nothing of the fearsomeness of the great lumbering contraptions of by-gone days. It was a replica in miniature: it was 'mustered' from three small margarine tubs filled with inflammable material, and nailed to a 'hatch' to which was fixed the orthodox drag chain. All that was needed to make the re-incarnation complete, were the old sack dresses of the Tar-barrel crew but, apparently, the 'boys' had not thought of this touch of realism. It was set ablaze and rushed round the town. A touch of pathetic humour was added by the display of a large black-edged placard bearing the words IN MEMORIAM. The hearts of many an old Lerwegian warmed at the sight of this reminder of the days of his youth, and a thrill went through him as he visualised the battles of days gone by.

Our old friend, the Editor of the *Shetland Times*, must have had an ineradicable streak of pessimism in his outlook on guizing. On Christmas Eve and New Year's Eve, 1891, there were not many Peerie Guizers abroad, but such as there were, "were very tastefully dressed, but they get less in number every year, and it seems as though this form of visitation was doomed to 'go under' in a short time". There was still, however, a number of older guizers who made their appearance after ten o'clock on Christmas Eve, and who continued their rounds until between seven and eight next morning.

A big effort was made at this time to renew interest in New Year's Eve guizing. To revive this interest, it was publicly announced that the squads should assemble at the Market Cross at eleven o'clock on New Year's Eve, form themselves into marching order, and, headed by the Town Band, have a procession along Commercial Street. This was done : the procession was lighted by six torches, twice perambulated through the Street and returned to the Cross where a merry dance was joined in to the strains of the bagpipes. The dance finished, the Band played the National Anthem, and, immediately the midnight hour had struck, the Band broke into 'A Guid New Year'. Another interesting item, on this occasion, was that the tower of the Town Hall was lighted up for the first time.

Up-Helly-Aa 1892 produced some improvements, one fiasco and one incident. The improvements consisted in the provision of coloured lights and Roman candles which were lighted at intervals during the procession. There was also a change in the 'make-up' of the Norse Galley. Not only was it gaily decorated but there was also built on the stern an artistic deckhouse in which were seated a number of fiddlers. A Long-ship with an artistic deckhouse aft seems at variance with the popular conception of the long, low Viking ship-of-war, but this apparently somewhat frivolous super-structure did at least have some historical justification as it was customary for Viking vessels and long-ships to have a tilt or awning, stretched over supports, under which the crew lived when not actually cruising. The deckhouse of this particular Galley was almost the means of sending the Galley to Valhalla before its final cruise had commenced. While the torches were being lighted, one of them came in contact with the ornate drapings, and set them alight. The flames shot up, and the fiddlers shot out, but the blaze was extinguished before much damage was done.

The Committee of Management was keen on making this procession as spectacular as possible, but they were rather too ambitious when they decided that it should be led by two guizers on horseback. One would like to think that their intention was to depict two raven-crested Jarls, arrayed in shining mail with flowing sheepskin mantles, and equipped with great battle-axes and daggers, proudly leading back their victorious Vikings from some far-flung foray, but, alas, the riders were only guizers in unspecified costumes, and their steeds declined to lead or to be led—at least, not in the van. 'When the band begins to play, my feet begin to go' runs the ode of the gentleman who loved to dance the polka, and when the band did begin to play, the two steeds commenced a polka which bade fair to wreck the procession. Their riders did their best to control them, but when they charged through the procession, the guizers signified that they had had enough equestrian displays, and the two 'mounted warriors' were ignominiously relegated to the rear, but even this humble position was too much for the horses, and they were returned to their stables.

The incident was an astute attempt to revive the Tar-barrel. A short time before the torchlight procession was due to start, a squad of seven guizers, each carrying a lighted torch, entered the Street from the Garrison Close, dragging behind them a model of a Tar-barrel with one tub, inside which was seated a certain Chief Constable. The effigy carried a placard on which were the words TAR-BARREL. Little did the Specials think as they nudged one another and chuckled at the all too apparent likeness—who could mistake these red whiskers?—that the tub was full of tar and chips or that the effigy, itself, was stuffed with shavings saturated with paraffin. Through the streets they marched till they came to the old turning spot at the Cockstool where they set fire to the effigy with their torches, and raced back. They had got as far as the Cross when their progress was stopped by a number of Specials who seized the Tar-barrel, dragged it down to the pier and tipped it into the sea.

Altogether, the Up-Helly-Aa of 1892 was by far the most successful, so far held, in organisation and brilliance. The dresses, too, were varied and well designed, especially those of a number of Eastern Ladies and a squad of Gondoliers.

The episode of the two steeds seems to have whetted the desires of some of the guizers to stage further equestrian displays, for, on the following Up-Helly-Aa, there appeared at the head of the procession, just behind the band, a group of clowns 'mounted' on horses. The wearers of the motley had gone to no end of trouble to make their appearance a success. The dresses were excellent, and their multi-coloured home-made 'mounts' carried them bravely throughout the route, while the antics of the whole squad caused great amusement to the spectators. The display was, undoubtedly, a sly skit on the previous year's fiasco.

There was no Norse Galley in 1893, but in its place was a model of a lighthouse on which was a placard with the inscription BROONIE'S TAING, and at the foot "Sacred to the Memory of the Balance of the Whale Fund". One can only guess at the meaning of this topical allusion. Some time previously a school of caain' whales had been driven ashore and killed at Hoswick by the fishermen and crofters of the district. The laird claimed his share as landlord. The fishermen denied his right to a share of the whales, and the case went before the Courts. The laird lost. Apparently a balance must have been left over from a fund raised to fight the case, and it may be that a suggestion had been made and turned down that the balance should be spent on erecting a lighthouse at Broonie's Taing. At the time, the case raised a tremendous amount of local interest, but why the Lerwick guizers should have substituted a 'lighthouse' and an 'In Memoriam' for the Norse Galley at Up-Helly-Aa is hard to understand.

In 1894 the Galley was once more included in the procession. It was 12 feet in length and four in breadth, and rested on a stand mounted on wheels, the stand being draped and painted to represent the sea. It is said to have been a magnificent model, but no further details are given. This is unfortunate as it would have been a matter of interest to have traced the yearly improvements and artistic developments which culminated in the really magnificent galleys of later years.

The steeds of 1892 were once again caricatured; this time by two guizers on hobby-horses who acted as escort to the Galley, and delighted the onlookers with their antics. The two leaders of the procession carried three-headed torches, and had a bodyguard of six torchbearers. These preceded the Galley, which was followed by the Band and two long lines of guizers, there being in all 120 torches. The most outstanding squads represented 'Mephistopheles', 'Sisters of Mercy', 'Bluebeard's Wives' and a Judge in ermine who was accompanied by his Bar of full-robed Barristers.

We are fortunate in having full details of the Balance Sheet of the 1894 procession. Here they are :—

CHARGE.

Total amount of subscriptions, conform to
    Subscription List £9 9 8

DISCHARGE.

Cost of 120 torches including materials and making, conform to vouchers			3	7	5
Cost of Norse Galley including materials and making, conform to vouchers			2	11	$9\frac{1}{2}$
Cost of fire-works, conform to vouchers ...				13	6
Sundries				6	$11\frac{1}{2}$
Balance of £2 10s, disposed of as follows:—					
Lerwick Brass Band	£1	0	0		
Gymnasium	0	15	0		
Sick Aid Society	0	15	0		
				2	10	0
				£9	9	8

Torches at 6¾d each appear cheap but are not unduly so when one remembers the cost of materials and labour in the early Nineties, but what of the 'Magnificent Norse Galley' at £2 11/9½? It can only be assumed that the greater part of the materials had been gifted, and that the main items of expense were for canvas and paint. The early galleys were constructed mostly from old rowing boats which were 'done up' for the occasion, and all the work in connection with making them was executed by the guizers themselves. Still, one can only marvel that, including the donation to the Band, a procession with 120 torches, fireworks and a galley, was successfully carried through at a total cost of £8. Why! the cost of a modern galley, alone, would be eight or nine times the total cost of the 1894 procession.

From now onwards, Up-Helly-Aa had definitely ousted Christmas and New Year which up to now had been the principal guizing nights. Squad-guizing at Christmas lingered on till the end of the century, but by 1896 First Fittin' had replaced guizing on New Year's Eve, and the Peerie Guizers

had, more and more, usurped Christmas Eve as their own
particular perquisite.   Later, New Year's Eve also was
claimed by them.   When first indulged in, there is little doubt
but that Peerie Guizing was started by the universal desire
of all children to ape their elders, and, when peerie Tammie
or peerie Baabie—da peerie jewels—masqueraded before
Granny, what more natural than that Granny should give
them a penny?   Children are quick to sense any scheme which
they think will merit reward, and it would not have taken them
long to realise that Peerie Guizing had the possibilities of an
El Dorado.   Kind relatives, in addition to Granny, would fall
under the spell of the youthful masqueraders, and, of course,
a quite casual call on the family grocer might be productive
of largesse, till the day arrived when every band of Peerie
Guizers, in their ones, twos and threes, armed with their poke,
called on house and shop alike and 'pleeped' out in high
falsetto tones their universal request of "Onythin' ta gie me da
night"?   So they claimed New Year's Eve, too, and with
it doubled their prospect of lucrative gains, and few there be
who can resist their plaintive appeal or refuse to add yet another
penny, orange, apple or cake to the poke.   Quite a few of
the Peerie Guizers go to no end of trouble to act the guizer's
part and don good costumes, but, to the majority, a blackened
face or non-descript garment is all that is considered necessary
to transform the youngsters into predatory mendicants bent on
mercenary gain.

        With the decline of Christmas guizing, due in large part
to the fact that very few houses 'opened', there came into
being a phase of guizing which called forth the censure of the
Press.   Bands of youths who made a pretence of guizing on
Christmas Eve "decked themselves out in unsightly attire and,
armed with a fog horn or that still more distressing instrument,
the accordion, paraded the streets, singly or in pairs, making
the night hideous".

Up-Helly-Aa 1895 was uneventful : there was a procession and a galley ; a large number of houses were 'open', and the guizers had a very successful night.

Up till now, the Committee of Management—it still went by that name—had advertised the procession by placing a placard at the Market Cross or sending round the bellman. In 1896 they went a step further and announced the arrangements for the procession in the *Shetland Times* and *Shetland News*. As the announcement marks a milestone in the ordered control of the festival, it is given in full :—

FESTIVAL OF UP-HELLY-A'.
GRAND TORCHLIGHT PROCESSION.

We are requested by the Committee to publish the following official programme of the Up-Helly-A' festivities :—

The squads will meet at the Market Cross on Wednesday evening, the 29th inst., at 7 o'clock sharp.

Each squad will be numbered, and will take up its position in the procession, two deep, according to its number. When this has been done, each guizer will be supplied with a torch, and the guizers are specially requested to remain in the places allotted to them, during the distribution of the torches, thus avoiding much confusion and delay. The word will then be given to light up, and the procession, headed by the galley, will proceed north through Commercial St., up Harbour St., south along High St. and Hillhead, down Queen's Lane, south through Commercial St. till Leog is reached, when the procession will turn and proceed north until opposite the Queen's Hotel, where a short halt will be made. The procession, headed by the band, will then march to the Market Cross, and form in a circle round the galley. After singing a verse of "Auld Lang Syne", the torches will be thrown into the galley.

When the procession starts, the band will play "The Hardy Norseman", and the guizers are requested to assist by singing the following :—

The Norseman's home in days gone by
    Was on the rolling sea,
And there his pennon did defy
    The foe of Normandy.
Then let us ne'er forget the race,
    Who bravely fought and died,
Who never filled a craven's grave,
    But ruled the foaming tide.

The noble spirits, bold and free,
    Too narrow was their land,
They roved the wide expansive sea,
    And quelled the Norman band.
Then let us all in harmony
    Give honour to the brave,
The noble, hardy, northern men,
    Who ruled the stormy wave.

The Norseman's power is past and gone,
    Their courage, strength and pride:
For now Britannia's sons alone,
    In triumph stem the tide;
Then may Victoria rule the land,
    Our laws and rights defend.
One cheer then give with heart and hand—
    The Queen!—the people's friend.

The squads will be supplied with their numbers on
applying to the Committee on or before Tuesday first, the
28th inst.

The Committee hope that each guizer will consider it his
duty to assist them in keeping order and making the procession
as successful as possible.

As clear-cut orders nothing could have been more concise
than the foregoing announcement, but it is remarkable in more
ways than one, for not only did it lay down the official

programme on which all orders for future Up-Helly-Aa processions were based, but it introduced the first organised singing, and singing has been an integral part of the programmes ever since.

The Galley of 1896 had the honour of being the first to have a mast fitted amidships, and from it there flew the Raven banner of the Viking Rovers.

The spectacular beauty of this procession was marred by a strong gale which played havoc with the torches. While going up Harbour Sreet, no less than forty heads fell off by reason of the sticks having been burned through, and, by the time the procession had finished its march, there were hardly enough torches left alight to start the bonfire. Another misfortune was the loss of one of the Galley's wheels which necessitated it leaving the procession at the top of Bank Lane, down which it was hauled back to the Cross. Still, 'all's well that ends well' : the bonfire was splendid; there was a large number of houses 'open', and the guizers had a glorious night.

The introduction of singing songs at Up-Helly-Aa must have inspired J. J. Haldane Burgess to give the guizers a song which they might claim as their very own. Burgess was a very fervent son of the 'Old Rock', and he may have felt that the last verse of "The Norseman's Home", in stating that 'The Norseman's power is past and gone, their courage, strength and pride', was somewhat derogatory to the descendants of the Vikings; but, whatever the reason, in January, 1897—he produced a stirring song which he dedicated to Up-Helly-Aa, and expressed the wish that it be sung at the festival processions. It was sung to the tune of "John Brown's Body" until 1921, when Mr Thomas Manson, Editor of the *Shetland News,* specially composed the fine swinging tune with which it has ever since been associated.

UP-HELLY-AA SONG.

From grand old Viking centuries Up-Helly-Aa has come,
Then light the torch and form the march, and sound the
  rolling drum;
And wake the mighty memories of heroes that are dumb;
    The waves are rolling on.

Chorus—

  Grand old Vikings ruled upon the ocean vast,
  Their brave battle-songs still thunder on the blast;
  Their wild war-cry comes aringing from the past;
      We answer it ''A-oi''!
  Roll their glory down the ages,
  Sons of warriors and sages,
  When the fight for Freedom rages,
      Be strong and bold as they!

Of yore, our fiery fathers sped upon the Viking Path;
Of yore, their dreaded dragons braved the ocean in its wrath;
And we, their sons, are reaping now their glory's aftermath;
    The waves are rolling on.

In distant lands, their raven-flag flew like a blazing star;
And foreign foemen, trembling, heard their battle-cry afar;
And they thundered o'er the quaking earth, those mighty
  men of war;
    The waves are rolling on

On distant seas, their dragon-prows went gleaming, outward
  bound;
The storm-clouds were their banners, and their music. ocean's
  sound;
And we, their sons, go sailing still the wide earth round and
  round;
    The waves are rolling on.

We are the sons of mighty sires, whose souls were staunch
and strong;
We sweep upon our serried foes, the hosts of Hate and
Wrong;
The glory of a grander Age has fired our battle-song;
The waves are rolling on.

Our galley is the People's Right, the dragon of the free;
The Right that, rising in its might, brings tyrants to their knee;
The flag that flies above us is the Love of Liberty;
The waves are rolling on.

In the processions of 1897 and 1898, banners were
carried aloft by some of the squads, and on these banners were
pointed allusions to topical events. For instance, in 1897 the
Worthy Chief Guizer had a banner on which were engraven
curious devices—probably tea-mugs—, and a placard on which
caustic references were made to an acrimonious dispute which
had occurred between the choir of the Auld Kirk and its
minister. The dispute was due to the minister ordaining that
the choir who contributed the musical part of the programme
should pay for their tickets of admission to the soiree but,
indignity of indignities, should take their own mugs with them !
The heat engendered in the community over this affair was
intense, and it was the main topic of wit and repartee to the
'aff-layers' during the visitations. In 1898 the banners were
inscribed with references to the affairs of the School Board and
the Burgh Sanitary Inspector, but these topics did not lend
themselves to caricature quite so well as did the 'affair of
the mugs'.

One other interesting item, in connection with the 1898
Up-Helly-Aa, was the first attempt at illuminating the placard
which, from the pillar at the Market Cross, notified the
guizers of the orders for the organisation of the procession.
These orders were re-inforced in the afternoon by the bellman,
who announced that the shops would close at seven o'clock,

that the guizers would assemble at seven-thirty, and that the procession would move off at eight.

This chapter opened with the record of the first galley introduced into the Up-Helly-Aa processions, and its close might be appropriately devoted to a few observations on the galley itself.

The first galleys, although at the time they were considered magnificent, were crude and poor when compared with those of later years, but, as the builders gained more experience and greater knowledge, we find a steady improvement in their design and embellishments. One must bear in mind that the Norse Galley, as depicted in the processions, is of heraldic rather than utilitarian design. No ship designed after the manner of the Up-Helly-Aa Long-ship could have 'worked to win'ward' in the most favourable breeze, and no rudder could ever have held her head into 'the eye of the wind' encumbered with the huge dragon head which adorns her prow. For those, then, who have never been privileged to look upon the 'Ancient Norse Galley' which lends dignity and splendour to all Up-Helly-Aa processions, we give the following brief description.

No longer are old rowing boats used : the galley is built throughout, plank by plank, by skilled ship-carpenters. The latest dimensions shew it to be twentyeight feet in length and about six in breadth, and it rests, as did the first galleys, on a billowy sea of painted canvas waves, the whole being borne on a very modern chassis and wheels of a discarded motor lorry.

The ship, itself, is a long low-waisted craft whose prow is in the shape of a bosom from which arises a long, scaly swanlike neck crowned with a dragon head of huge proportions. The head is really a work of art—great gaping mouth adorned with fangs and beard and long forked tongue ; wide open nostrils from which, at any moment, one might expect to see the fiery breath belch forth ; fierce staring eyes and fiercer mane, and all most realistically painted in deep vermilion, black, white and silver or gold. At the stern, as if to counterbalance the head, rises a massive fishlike tail, fashioned and coloured after the style of the head and neck. Spaced along the sides, are fastened the shields of the warriors, each bearing in diverse designs the arms of the Vikings. By each shield is an oar whose handle passes through the gunwale, and whose blade is buried deep in the billowy sea. Over the bows hang the anchors, and from the bosom of the prow[35] projects the gatelike ram which was used to shatter the hulls of opposing Long-ships. From amidships rises the single mast which carries the great square sail, now furled on its yard with all the cordage fastened to the gunwales. Above the square sail, encircling the mast, is the cagelike crow's-nest, and topping all flies the raven-emblazoned flag of the old Viking Rovers. Forward of the mast and close to the prow, stands the spar bearing aloft a crimson hand, and, finally, through the starboard quarter projects the long steering oar[36]. Each galley is painted according to tradition, and bears a name which has been culled from Norse lore or borne by a Dragon-ship famous in history. Seen in the hard bright light of day, it is wonderful, but, under the glare of the torches and with the mail-clad Jarl, battle-axe in hand, standing on the quarterdeck, it is truly magnificent.

What is the significance of the blood-red hand which stands up so conspicuously between the mast and the prow?

---

[35]The prow and stern of Viking vessels were not bosom-shaped. They curved upwards and outwards high above the level of the waist of the ship. Authorities say that in some cases, if not all, the dragonhead and tail were removable, and that they were stowed away when cruising.

[36]The Viking ships were not steered with an oar. They had a rudder shaped like a short-bladed oar which hung perpendicularly over the starboard quarter, and was held in position by a wooden bracket attached to the hull. A rope with a knot on the end was passed through a hole in the rudder and a corresponding hole in the bracket, and was made fast inside the hull. The neck of the rudder was secured to the gunwale with a grommet, and the steering was done by a tiller which fitted at right angles into the rudder above the grommet.

One explanation is that it was a sort of battle-ensign which was raised aloft when a Long-ship went into action. But why a blood-red hand? Was not the Raven Banner battle-ensign enough to all who sailed the 'Viking Path'? If bald, prosaic history does not vouchsafe to us the reason, let us turn, then, to the legend which relates how two Long-ships were cruising towards the west when land was sighted—one version of the legend claims that the land was an island in Shetland while another maintains that the island was in the Faroes, and so on. Hardly had the lookout's hail of "Land ahead!" died away than the two ships leapt into life and started racing towards it, for by tradition whichever Jarl first touched the land, his it was by right. The Vikings bent to their oars, and a bow wave rose in front of the prows; side by side they swept on; now, one would draw ahead, only to be overtaken by the other as the Jarl chided and spurred the oarsmen to greater effort. Then with fierce taunts and curses each crew strove to out-race the other, but to neither came any outstanding lead; the shore loomed up ahead but now, except for the oaths of the Jarls and the great gulping breaths of the oarsmen, the crews were silent; the muscles on their backs and arms rose in knots and fell again as the Vikings drove the ships through the water. Still, there was no decisive lead, and it looked as if both prows would grind upon the sand at the same moment. Then it was that one of the Jarls laid his arm on the deck, and with his sword struck off his left hand at the wrist. Seizing the severed hand with his right he flung it far ashore before his rival's prow had grated on the sand. His hand had touched the new land; his title was established. So, ever after, the Vikings commemorated this epic contest by flaunting aloft a blood-red hand on their Long-ships whenever they set out on forays bent or joined issue with some hostile craft.

CHAPTER XVII.

TO be punctiliously correct the title of this chapter should be The Proclamation, but it is doubtful if one guizer in a hundred would recognise THE BILL by that name. To everyone it is just the Bill, and the Bill has become one of the most important features of Up-Helly-Aa.

Its primary purpose was to give final instructions to the guizers about the time, formation and route of the procession and any other details decreed by The Worthy Chief Guizer or, as he later became, The Guizer Jarl. The Bill replaced the Proclamation which was attached to the pillar of the Market Cross on Up-Helly-Aa mornings prior to 1899.

The first part of the Bill follows the lines of the old Proclamation, that is, it gives the general information which the guizers and the public require to know about the arrangements for the procession; but the remainder is devoted to the 'jokes'. These are compiled by the Jokes Committee, whose members are elected annually from the Guizers' Committee. For obvious reasons their names are not made public, but, except that new blood is added from time to time, the same members serve on the Jokes Committee year after year. This is very necessary as the art of phrasing the 'jokes' is not one that can be acquired without long experience.

The jokes are all topical, and deal with events, public and private, in the lives of the citizens throughout the previous year. Mostly the 'jokes' are of such a nature that the victim can thoroughly enjoy 'being in the Bill', but hard hitting is also indulged in, and on more than one occasion the castigation administered has almost led to actions for defamation of character. 'Where there is smoke, there is fire', and, although threatening letters have passed, no action for defamation has ever been taken to a Court of Law. Perhaps just as well !

The first Bill made its appearance in 1899. No copy of its contents has been preserved, but we have it on record that "touching with a keen sense of humour on local events, the production was decidedly clever, and it is to be regretted that the distinctly personal allusions which it contained prevent its reproduction".

There is no record of a Bill in 1900, and, owing to the death of Queen Victoria, the 1901 festival was cancelled. In 1902 a Bill with a small number of 'jokes' was again displayed at the Market Cross, and from that year onwards the Bill became an integral part of the festival. The quality of the 'jokes' in 1902 is not very high but, thereafter, not only do the 'jokes' increase in number but they improve in style and point as the Jokes Committee gained experience.

A copy of the Bill exhibited in 1905 is reproduced at the end of this chapter. It is not so involved as some of those of later years, and can, with footnotes, be made intelligible to the reader, and will serve to illustrate the type of humour inseparable from the Bill. After a lapse of forty years, the author may be forgiven if he fails to explain some of the 'jokes' correctly or to guess at the meaning of others.

If one is not conversant with the incidents on which the 'jokes' are based, they can convey no meaning unless someone volunteers an explanation, and only then do they become really funny or humorous to the individual in a small town where everyone knows the idiosyncrasies and doings of everybody else. Take this more obvious sample culled from the Bill of 1910. (In the Bill the words or letters to be emphasised are printed in italics or red ink, but to make them more distinct, they are shewn here in small capital letters). "The SKATING RINK has fairly FLOORED the Good Templars; many have become BACKSLIDERS and taken to D'RINK". A roller-skating rink had been started in the town, and this had seriously affected the attendances at the meetings of the Good Templars. The Templars had made quite a fuss about the backsliding of their members. The Jokes Committee was not slow to exploit the situation.

The text of the Bill almost invariably ends with a Penalty Clause, of which this was one : "Defacers of this Bill will be struck by a COLLIE CLUB as all MONGRELS are entitled to be". In the years round about 1908, there was a craze for so-called Shetland Collies which were bred from a real Shetland Collie and a Pekinese Lap Dog. The result was not unlike a very pretty diminutive collie, but the Dog Clubs declined to recognise this mongrel, and the Jokes Committee was gifted with a pungent Penalty Clause.

Bills are signed "BY ORDER and under the Seal of the GUIZER JARL". The seal is a large one in red wax and bears the motto "We axe for What we Want" and a battle axe. Up to 1905 the Bill was signed by THE WORTHY CHIEF GUIZER whose seal was the imprint of a human foot inserted between the words "His Mark".

The Bill is pasted on a hoarding measuring roughly ten feet high and six wide. The first information we have in regard to decoration is in 1898, when the Proclamation was described as a 'huge coloured poster'. Thereafter, till 1909, it is variously described as 'striking', 'artistic' and so on. In 1909 the first of the water-colour paintings appeared on the head of the Bill. The subject was a finely executed painting of a

Norse Long-ship. Each year, thereafter, the Bill was emblazoned with Long-ships, a Viking Jarl lying in state on his blazing Long-ship carrying him to Valhalla, Vikings carousing round a groaning board, to mention a few of the paintings. The other decorations of the Bill included heraldic designs, armorial bearings and intricate scrolls and traceries, but no decoration was complete without a Long-ship.

The Guizers' Committee has always been fortunate in being able to call on talented local artists whose souls were steeped in Nordic lore, and who had the ability to make their pictures living and realistic. Peter Martin was responsible for the original colouring of the Proclamations. James M. Smith was the first to paint the Long-ships. He was followed by Fred Irvine, R. S. W. Paterson, William Johnson, Jr., A. W. S. Coutts. and Tom Henry. Mr Henry has been the official artist for a number of years, and undoubtedly, for variety in choice of subject and the super-excellence of his work, he has been the most outstanding of a team of brilliant craftsmen. His paintings have deserved a better fate than to be buffeted and torn by the weather and cast away at the end of the day.

We must not leave the subject of decorative painting without paying tribute to that highly talented artist Arthur Abernethy, who since 1906 has been responsible for painting scenes on the heads of the Collecting Sheets. The Collecting Sheets are always in the form of a scroll setting forth an appeal to The Worthy Burghers of Lerwick. A sample of a Collecting Sheet has already been given, and, except for the yearly change of phraseology and reference to current events, it has kept the same lay-out from year to year. Mr Abernethy's paintings are all gems of art. They, too, depict Viking scenes in widely different settings. One of his spirited pictures shows two hostile Long-ships sailing in to attack the Pictish Broch on Mousa. On the ships stand the Vikings ready to leap ashore, while ashore one of the garrison is running to raise the alarm. The vivid painting of the Vikings, the sea, the rocky shore and the broch is a delightful piece of realistic art.   Mr Abernethy's

work has fared better than that of Mr Henry, as most of the Collecting Sheets are now preserved in the Library.

To return to the Bill, the collection of 'jokes' is not confined to the Committee.   It is rather an accumulation gathered throughout the year and filed away till required. When some incident, ludicrous, venomous or topical, occurs, it is no uncommon thing to hear the remark "That's good enough for the Bill", and invariably some member of the Committee earmarks it for future reference.   By the time the Committee meets to prepare the script, there is usually more subject-matter than can possibly be utilised.   The painting and decoration of the Bill is done beforehand so that when the Committee meet on the evening before Up-Helly-Aa they can start right away on the 'jokes'.   The printer, perched on a table with his brushes and his black and red inks, is ready to transcribe the 'jokes' to the Bill as they are handed up to him. It is related how on one occasion, when Peter Martin was artist, there was a long pause while two of the Committee wrangled over the suitability of a 'joke'. Peter, for want of anything better to do, sketched in the head of a man with a rather enigmatical expression on his countenance in the space where the next 'joke' should have gone. The appearance of this head on the Bill was, for days afterwards, a fruitful subject for speculation as to which member of the community it caricatured, and many essays were made to fit an appropriate hat on it. It was somewhat of an anticlimax when the truth was divulged.

Each member discloses his stock of promising 'joke' material. Some of it has already been framed in Bill phraseology or in doggerel rhyme, and the Committee settles down to separate the dross from the gold. Any Jokes Committeeman will tell you that the gold always contains many 'jokes' of such superlative piquancy that they dare not be exposed to the public gaze. Except where it is deliberately intended to administer castigation the Committee does try to refrain from giving offence. While they are selecting and framing the 'jokes', the printer occupies the time filling in the general instructions to the guizers, and by the time this is completed the first lot of 'jokes' is ready for transcribing. By midnight the work is well forward and the members adjourn for refreshment : hot pies, coffee and beer help to renew their energies, and back to work they go. By four or five o'clock in the morning the Bill is completed and the seal attached. Only one thing more has to be done—carry the hoarding to the Market Cross and attach it securely to the pillar ; then home to snatch a few hours' sleep before tackling another day of arduous preparation and a still more arduous night of revelling.

The following is the text of the Bill of 1905 :—

UP-HELLY-A'.

GRAND TORCHLIGHT PROCESSION.

I, the undersigned, hereby give forth that the Guizers will assemble at the South Esplanade at 7.30 p.m.; procession to start at 8 prompt from the Market Cross, and follow the time-honoured route. For further particulars read the NORSEMAN'S DAILY MAIL[37].

Our Galley, certified to carry 12 PASSENGERS[37], will be cleared by the Worthy Chief Guizer SHAN-HIS-EE[38] at the Custom House.

The solution of the unemployed problem will be found at the head of the Galley which will not be drawn by the CO-OPERATIVE DIVIDEND but by ordinary TREADERS[39].

Guizers carrying SMALL POCKS will be KNABBED and disinfected with CHICKEN LYMPH[40].

Guizers with CROOKED SHANKS[41] will be permitted to hold on to the handrails coming down the lanes.

Scalloway Guizers are requested to take a SMA DRINK of the LERWICK MILK to augment their WATER SUPPLY[42].

Any Town Councillor caught fishing with a COUNTY ROD[43] at the new FISH QUAY[44] will receive CORPORAL PUNISHMENT[45] at the hands of the Lerwick School Board.

The MOTOR CAR SERVICE presently running through the Press is GAAN SOON to run through the COUNTY R.D.[46].

All fishermen requiring BAIT are requested to call at the Gymnasium for MUSSELS. Ladies from the Gymnasium taking part in the procession must not HALT on the way[47].

No small ray of UNROMANTIC LIGHT will be shed by us on LONE LOVERS[48].

County Councillors can have their teeth withdrawn without a Poll by a J.P. in the CENTRAL WARD[49].

The W.C.G. being opposed to gambling, this bill (which has been VULCANISED[50] and will not burn) will be RAFFLED in the BAPTIST KIRK[51] in aid of the LIBERAL ASSOCIATION[52].

After the Procession the Guizers will circle round the Galley and join the Directors of the Old and New Companies[37] in singing

"The Norseman's home in days gone by,
Was on the rolling sea".

Defacers of this Bill will be trawled A.LANG[52] to the GENTLE ANNIEmosity[53] of the Junior Bailie[54].

Given under my hand and seal this last day of the Festival.

The Worthy Chief Guizer.

His   Mark.

For the purpose of elucidation the 'jokes' have been numbered :—

37—Refers to the steamship *Norseman* which had been acquired by a local Company to compete with The North of Scotland & Orkney & Shetland Steam Navigation Company. The local Company was agitating to get a Post Office Mail Contract. As against the North Steamers' large passenger accommodation the *Norseman* held a certificate allowing her to carry twelve passengers only. In the final instructions to the Guizers about singing, the Bill cleverly associates the Directors of both Companies who were at daggers drawn.

38—Is a play on the name of the Supervisor of Customs,

Shaughnessy, in Shetland dialect, SHAN (shewing)—HIS (his)—EE (eye).

39—Refers to the newly-formed Co-operative Society and the local Traders who were strongly opposing it.

40—A case diagnosed as smallpox had been isolated in the Knab isolation hospital, and there had been the consequent spate of vaccinations. Later the "smallpox" turned out to be Chickenpox, hence the reference to Chicken Lymph.

41—The Town Council had just fitted handrails to the walls of the lanes under the supervision of the Burgh Surveyor, Mr Cruikshank.

42—The people in various districts in Shetland, as in other parts of the kingdom, have their local soubriquets, such as 'Lerwick Whitin's', 'Whalsay Piltiks' and 'Deltin' Spaarls'; so in the same way the Scallowegians are known as 'Scalloway Sma Drink'. There had been complaints about the water content of the Lerwick milk which the W.C.G. suggests might be drawn upon to augment the new Water Supply Scheme for Scalloway.

43—Not understood. Probably refers to some discussion on the need for more County roads.

44—Plans for a new Fish Quay were under discussion.

45—Refers to heated arguments in the School Board on the subject of corporal punishment in the schools.

46—Messrs Ganson Bros. were trying to establish a motor car service in the County, and the project had been freely discussed in the Press. "Rd." being the abbreviation for "road", play is being made on Mr R. D. Ganson's initials.

47—There had been trouble over the fishermen raiding the mussel beds for bait. According to the W.C.G. there was a good supply to be had at the Gymnasium where some of the ladies' class received injuries which caused them to halt (limp).

48—The Town Council in erecting a gas-lamp in the Lovers' Loan had called forth jocular criticism of their unsympathetic action. The Guizers, of course, would never have been guilty of such 'unromantic' behaviour! The Lovers' Loan is the road stretching from St. Magnus Rectory (formerly the House of Charity) in Knab Road down to the Widows' Homes.

49—Reference to criticism of the election of Mr J. P. Henderson,

Dentist, to the County Council without the seat being contested   The word 'Poll' is a subtle quip on the dentist's ability to 'pull'.

50—''Vulcanised''—reference obscure.

51—Members of the Baptist Church were prominent in condemning raffles.

52—Evidently in connection with an appeal for funds for the Liberal Association, of which Mr A. L. Laing was Chairman.   Mr Laing was also prominent in conjunction with Mr Wason, M.P., in moving for better detection and prosecution of illegal trawling.

53—The soubriquet of a local policeman.

54—Mr A. L. Laing.

CHAPTER XVIII.

THE Up-Helly-Aa Festival, having acquired its Torches, its Galley, its own Song and the Bill, may now be said to have got over the years of childhood. It had been born in turbulence, had had many teething troubles and a good many childish illnesses. Many times the Sun-God must have despaired of seeing his offspring survive, but survive it did and waxed in strength so that towards the end of the century it had become quite a sturdy child which was just entering on its adolescence. Like every healthy adolescent youngster, it sought to break new ground, tried out new ideas, and discarded many.

No longer did the City Fathers frown on the activities of the guizers; rather was it very much the other way. It was no uncommon thing to find members of the Town Council, lawyers and elders of the kirk out with the squads on Up-Helly-Aa, or, dressed in the garments of their grandparents—yes! both sexes!—first fittin' on New Year's morning. Even the Sheriff went out of his way to entertain the squads, and none made them more welcome than Sheriff Moffat. A few Special Police were still enrolled for the festive season, but beyond keeping a benevolent eye on the revellers and a watchful one

K

for any chance outbreak of fire due to burnt-off torch-heads, they had little to do.

The trade of the Town also benefited at a period of the year when business was very slack, for not only did the guizers spend a lot of money on dresses, and their hosts on entertaining, but Up-Helly-Aa drew crowds of country folk to the town. The county roads had been improved, and vehicular traffic had improved with them. The inter-island steamer *Earl of Zetland* served the islands, and the records shew that each year the *Earl* was full to capacity with spectators from the Isles. The Sun-god must have beamed with pleasure.

First Fittin' has already been described in Chapter XV, but during this period it became more popular than ever. The reason for this enthusiasm is not far to seek. First Fittin' had been the acknowledged perquisite of the men. It was customary for the ladies to remain at home to receive the First Fitters and to entertain them, but now they began to take an active interest in the positive side of guizing. There is one authenticated case of a damsel who, greatly daring, donned a male dress and took part in a Tar-barrel ploy in the early Eighties, but she took great care not to reveal the fact until long afterwards.

On New Year's Eve, 1901, there must have been a considerable amount of serious discussion on the part of a few ladies and probably a great deal of persuasion on the part of a like number of gentlemen, as to whether or not the ladies should dare to dress-up and accompany their swains 'first fittin'. Can't you hear them?

"Na, na! Lowrie, we cudna do it. Whit wid da folk tink? Tamar, du wid never do it, wid du?"

"Weel, Leebie, if du'll geng, A'm game".

"Dat's fine, Lasses, cum on".

"So! if Leebie's set on gaen, dan A'll cum tü; bit lass, I tink we'r daft".

But daft or not, several ladies did go 'first fittin' on New

Year's Morning, 1901, and not only did they have a grand time, but proved themselves as adept at 'aff-laying' as their escorts. There may have been some criticism of this rather bold departure from the Victorian standard of conduct expected from young ladies, but, if there were, it had no effect, as from then on hardly a Christmas or New Year has passed without a quota of lady-guizers. This new departure by the gentler sex was not long confined to the younger generation; married ladies and elderly spinsters were not slow to take advantage of this new-found freedom and the opportunity it gave them to give rein to their tongues from behind the security of their masks, but surely the peak of freedom was reached when three grannies donned guizing dresses, and unescorted did the rounds till 4 a.m. One was garbed in her wedding dress, another in garments that had belonged to her mother, while the third sported a frockcoat, striped trousers, tile hat and cane. They were certainly the most popular squad 'out' that night.

The ladies did not generally unmask unless their identity was established beyond doubt, which was a revival of the custom of the early days of guizing. When, however, an elderly lady, who had remained unidentified, did elect to take off her mask before her own special friends, she was invariably greeted with a chorus of an incredulous "You!" and roars of laughter. By far the funniest dénouement of this kind happened some years ago. A married lady decided to go 'first fittin' with some friends while her husband stayed at home. Not long after his wife's departure the husband was overcome by a desire to go guizing himself. He had been a great guizer in his youth and a past-master in the art of 'aff-lay'. He had no trouble in finding some garments which completely hid his identity, and off he set to make a few calls on his own. After visiting one or two houses, he overtook his wife and her squad enjoying themselves in the house of one of his closest friends. Now, the fun began : he knew his wife but she did not know

him or even dream that he would be so daft as to go guizing
at his time of life. She was a good 'aff-layer' but he was a
better, and, besides, had the most unfair advantage of knowing
all her private affairs. At first the 'aff-lay' took the usual
course of cross-talk and banter, but gradually the husband
began to slip in some quiet allusions to incidents which are
every-day occurrences in the course of a long married life, but
are not normally bruited abroad even to one's friends. The
lady was somewhat staggered, and her 'aff-lay' lost its
brilliance as she tried in vain to solve who this guizer could be
and how he could possibly have had the knowledge he
professed. There crept into her voice a touch of acerbity as
she countered his assertions, but the climax came when her
husband blandly referred to some glamorous episodes of their
courting days. This was too much for her, she turned about
and left him without so much as vouchsafing a retort. A few
minutes later the squad took off their masks. Everyone knew
who they were so there was no surprise, but what of this lone
guizer? Would he never unmask? But the lone guizer was
thoroughly enjoying the situation, and kept the company on
tenterhooks for some time longer, then quietly slipping off his
mask and grinning broadly, he revealed himself. His wife's
half angry, half laughing "You! I might ha' kent" was
hardly heard amid the peals of laughter.

Up-Helly-Aa, 1899, was notable for the introduction of
the Bill, but it had one other innovation which set a fashion
which was copied for a number of years. In addition to the
Norse Galley, there was introduced into the procession the first
model of a ship. In this instance it was something of a
caricature of the mail steamer *Queen*. In case the casual
onlooker should not recognise the familiar lines of the weekly
mail-boat, the name WHEEN was painted on her bows. To
those not conversant with the Shetland dialect, it is necessary to
explain that it is still quite common to sound the initial letters

'Qu' of a word as 'Wh'. The model caused a good deal of amusement but seemed to be more of a joke than anything else. The *Wheen* carried as passengers two old women (guizers) who kept up a lamentation over the remains of a broken spinning wheel—a topical allusion to an action in Court brought by a woman against the Superintendent of Police who, in company with a man, entered her house without a warrant and removed a spinning wheel. The Superintendent handed over the wheel to the man who claimed that it was his property, and not, as averred by the woman who had been his housekeeper, a gift from him to her. Sheriff Shennan decided in favour of the Superintendent —hence the lamentations. Later Sheriff-Principal Thoms reversed this judgement. The *Wheen's* bunting consisted of a number of banners bearing quips at the expense of the School Board.

In 1900 the Festival had to be postponed for a fortnight on account of a severe epidemic of influenza. When the procession did take place, it was quite successful, and an added attraction was the firing of coloured rockets from the s.s. *Earl of Zetland*. For the first time, too, the local Press published the name of the Worthy Chief Guizer—Mr J. W. Robertson. In spite of the success of the procession, the guizers had rather a poor night's fun as, owing to the influenza epidemic, very few houses were 'open'.

Up-Helly-Aa 1901 was cancelled on account of the death of Queen Victoria.

Although the festival was officially cancelled, there was quite a body of young men and women who were not in favour of such action, and thereby hangs a tale. A small committee was formed to sponsor an Up-Helly-Aa dance, and it was decided that invitations to it should be by cards rather than by advertisement which, more than likely, would offend public opinion.

One day a member of the Dance Committee called at the
office of the *Shetland Times,* and handed to the secretary—a
sister-in-law of the Editor—a card on which was written the
usual form of invitation, "The Up-Helly-Aa Dance Committee
requests the pleasure, etc." while on the left hand bottom corner
were the letters R.S.B.D. (It is said that actually the letters
were R.S.B.B. but for the purpose of telling this tale we prefer
R.S.B.D.). An order for the number of invitation cards
required was given together with instructions that the printing
was to be in gold lettering. Miss L. took a note of the order,
and then, as a matter of routine, checked over the wording of
the invitation. When her eyes lighted on the R.S.B.D., she
hesitated for a moment and then very tactfully remarked :—

"Excuse me, Mr A., but is this not a mistake, shouldn't
the letters be R.S.V.P. ?"

"Na, na ! Miss L. that may be your wye o't bit hit's no
wirs, an' you'll jist print the letters wir wye".

"Very well, Mr A., just as you say", and the letters
R.S.B.D. duly appeared on the invitation cards.

Miss L. was not the only one to question the correctness
of R.S.B.D. ; those who received the invitations were likewise
puzzled, and soon the members of the Dance Committee were
being interrogated as to what these letters signified, but not one
of them seemed inclined to elucidate matters. Requests to
people with a knowledge of French brought the solution no
nearer till one day a member of the Committee blurted out that
they did not see why the death of the Queen should be allowed
to interfere with Up-Helly-Aa, and that, at any rate, they were
going to have their dance, cancellation or no cancellation, and,
if his questioner really wanted to know what R.S.B.D. stood
for, well, it was Royal Sovereign Be Damned.

For long afterwards the Editor of the *Shetland Times*
never missed a chance in company to tease his sister-in-law by

asking her to tell the story of how she helped to inveigle the *Times* into committing an act of *lèse majesté*.

As if to make up for the abandonment of the Festival in the previous year, Up-Helly-Aa 1902 was a great success, and there was a large number of houses 'open' though some experiments were tried out which did not prove altogether successful. The guizers bearing torches numbered 80, but if everything had gone according to plan, there would have been a further 100 torches which would have made the procession a very striking one.

At this period of the year there were hundreds of Royal Naval Reserve men putting in their training in Fort Charlotte. It had been arranged that the 'Dreelers', as they were called, would join the procession with a Galley and 100 torches. The Guizers duly formed up at the appointed hour, but the 'Dreelers' failed to put in an appearance. After waiting for a time the Guizers 'lighted up' and set off with their Viking Ship at their head. At the tail-end of the procession bravely trudged some squads of juveniles headed by their own miniature galley. There had been a heavy fall of snow, and before long the Viking Ship plunged into a drift and remained fast. The procession carried on and left behind some men to find shovels to 'refloat' the Galley. In this they were successful, and the Galley later rejoined the procession at the tail-end.

Meanwhile, the 'Dreelers' had been having a ploy of their own. They had built a most elaborate galley representing Neptune's Car—the work of the naval instructors. Aboard sat Neptune on his throne surrounded by a bevy of sea-nymphs all gorgeously arrayed in flowing robes of sea-green and other gay colours. By way of adding a modern touch, they had also built a finely proportioned model of a torpedo-boat which, with its captain and crew aboard, made a brave show as it followed Father Neptune's carriage. The Navy has always been famous for the punctual fulfilment of its engagements, but on this

occasion the appearance of such marvellous craft in the square
of the Fort was too much for the 'Dreelers'. They went mad
with excitement, and soon hundreds of 'Dreelers' were
capering round the galleys in a sort of war-dance. By the
time they had quietened down, the Guizers' procession was
over, so they had a procession of their own, and, on reaching
the Market Cross, added their galleys to the embers of the
Viking Ship. Thus ended the one and only attempt at
collaboration between the Guizers' Committee and the
'Dreelers'.

Another innovation which was not authorised by the
Guizers' Committee, was the inclusion of a number of girls
among the squads in the procession. No doubt, the new-found
freedom and success of the lady 'first fitters' on New'r's Day
Morn 1901 had inspired a number of girls with the idea that,
if they could go out 'first fittin', there was no reason why they
should not go out with the guizers on Up-Helly-Aa. The
Committee put its foot down on this experiment, and, so far
as it is known, it was not repeated.

One other innovation was tried out, and proved very
successful. For years back the squads had been increasing in
size from the old Tar-barrel squad of seven to ten, twelve and
more, also the number of guizers had increased. Householders
found that the old-time kitchen could not accommodate the
increased numbers. Some did try to cater for larger squads by
throwing open more rooms, but it was becoming more and
more difficult to do justice to the Guizers in the way of providing
adequate dancing space or in the provision of refreshments.
Half-a-dozen ladies met to discuss the problem and decided
to hire the Rechabite Hall, to which could be invited their
friends and a number of girls as dancing partners for the
Guizers, while they and their maids would be free to deal with
the refreshments. The new venture turned out to be an
unqualified success in spite of protests by some of the older

guizers who averred that the abandonment of the homely hospitality of the 'open' house would kill the spirit of Up-Helly-Aa and all that it stood for. This question of the hiring of halls cropped up again at the Guizers' Meeting in January, 1903. The great majority of the guizers took the view that, owing to the large numbers now taking part in the Festival, it was impossible for householders to entertain them in their houses, and that, unless halls were utilised, very soon not a house would 'open'. Protests and opposition to the 'opening' of the halls soon petered out, and in a very few years entertaining in houses practically ceased, except in a few cases.

There is nothing of outstanding interest in the 1903 Festival, except that, in addition to the official Norse Galley, there was, in the procession, another built by lads from St. Magnus Street, and a fully-rigged schooner built by the Docks Boys. The latter, having been constructed by practical sailors and craftsmen, was a very fine effort which called forth great praise from old sea-dogs and land-lubbers alike. Both galleys and the schooner were manned by fiddlers.

The reader may well be excused if by now he complains— "You are continually telling us all about the processions and incidents, but, surely, the dresses worn by the Guizers are of some interest. Why not mention a few as you go along"? To give a detailed list of all the squads and their dresses would bore the reader to tears and read like a Sales Catalogue, but if a few are mentioned yearly, they will serve to shew the amazing versatility of the Guizers in their choice of costumes. Here, then, are a few picked from over twenty squads—200 guizers—which were 'out' in 1903 :—

Black and White	Pirates
The Scarlet Woman	The Woman in White
The Black Dwarf	The Manxman
The Queen of the Night	Night

The squad representing Night wore one of the most striking and impressive dresses ever worn at Up-Helly-Aa. The head-dresses consisted of close-fitting college caps, on the crown of each of which were three black rods, one in front bearing a silver crescent-moon, while those on either side bore silver stars. The masks were black velvet hoods which completely enveloped the head. Draped over the shoulders and reaching to the ground were loose-fitting black robes profusely decorated with silver moons and stars. In their black-gloved hands they carried a crook from which was suspended an antique square lantern lit by a carriage candle. The impressive grandeur of the appearance of this squad was greatly enhanced by the fact that more than half of them were six-footers. Being provided with lanterns, they did not carry torches in the procession.

The 1904 Festival was much the same as that of the previous year except that there does not seem to have been any extra galleys. There was one curious feature, however; the Worthy Chief Guizer was dressed in a beautiful velvet costume representing Hamlet. Why the 'Gloomy Dane' should have been selected to reign over the revels of Up-Helly-Aa is, at first sight, a little difficult to understand. Hamlet standing on the poop of a Viking long-ship is the very antithesis of a Viking Sea Rover. We must, however, keep in mind that, so far, Up-Helly-Aa was the night of nights of revelling, and that its trend towards the symbolism of ancient Nordic mythology and the reincarnation of Viking heroes, had only got as far as torches—symbolic of the Sacrificial Fires—and Viking ships. It can only be assumed that the Worthy Chief Guizer decided that Hamlet would be a striking and distinctive figure to grace the head of the procession.

The diehards having been decisively routed on the question of the 'opening' of halls, now found another cause for complaint. This time it centred round the preferential treatment of some squads in private houses. It so happened that the wife of one of the leading citizens, himself a guizer, had on two occasions provided a hot supper for her husband's squad, and, naturally, it had been arranged that the squad would make their visit about the time supper was ready. After they had had their ploy, they retired to the dining-room where they were entertained to an excellent meal and had a sing-song. All the other squads received their refreshments in the room set apart for this purpose. It was admitted that the provendor and drinks supplied were as good as, if not better than in the majority of the houses, but "why make fish of one and flesh of another?"; "from time immemorial guizers were all equal"; "the spirit of Up-Helly-Aa was being killed"; and so on. So ran the arguments of the diehards, never stopping to consider that if a lady wished to entertain her personal friends on Up-Helly-Aa night, that was her affair. The complaints were ignored, and the spirit of Up-Helly-Aa was *not* killed.

The following year, 1905, is noteworthy for several reasons. J. J. Haldane Burgess published the Up-Helly-Aa Song which appears earlier in this volume. The local Press awakened to the 'news' value of Up-Helly-Aa and the growing asset it was to the Town. They devoted almost three columns of newsprint to a description of the Festival; they published photographs of the Galley and the battleship, and they printed the Bill in full—rather a change from the previous maximum of a bare half column, and the miserable eight line paragraph in the Nineties. This year, too, saw the final appearance of the Worthy Chief Guizer and his Seal of Office, the impression of a human foot sandwiched between the words "His Mark". Mr McGowan Scott was the last of the Worthy Chiefs.

In addition to the Norse Galley, the Docks Boys produced a model of Admiral Togo's Flagship. It was a well-made model with 28 guns, all turned and hollowed out, torpedo tubes and nets, fighting-tops, wireless, searchlights and

Japanese flags. The publication of the photograph of the Galley enables us to compare the earlier models with those of later years. The photograph of this year's Galley depicts a somewhat dumpy ship rather overburdened with a huge dragon-head and tail. It had four shields only on either side but no oars or pole with the red hand on top. At the time these early models were quite justly considered magnificent, but they are puny when compared with the latest models.

How well the Guizers had established themselves with law and order is demonstrated by a telegram to the Worthy Chief Guizer from Sheriff Moffat, who was from home, wishing him and the Guizers a good Up-Helly-Aa, · and expressing the wish that some of the squads would visit Helendale (over a mile from Lerwick) where Mrs Moffat was expecting them.

Among the squads 'out' there were—

Heralds	African Warriors
Herring Gutters	Blue Beard and his Wives
Gymnasium Girls	Costermongers
Knight of the Plantagenet Period	Bill Bailey

At a mass meeting of the Guizers held in January, 1906, it was decided to drop the title Worthy Chief Guizer, and substitute the much more appropriate one of Guizer Jarl, and, in order that the Jarl should more realistically look the part, it was agreed to purchase a Viking suit of armour complete with raven-crested helmet and accoutrements. As this suit would be worn by successive Jarls—stout, thin and normal—the problem arose as to how this difficulty might be got over. It was solved by sewing the plates of mail on to a woollen jersey which clung to the figure of the Jarl of normal proportions and expanded to cling just a little more closely to the Jarl of Falstaffian girth.

From time to time there have been slight alterations to suit individual figures and tastes, but in all essential details the regalia of the Guizer Jarl remains constant—silver helmet with raven wings on either side, a corselet and sleeves of silver mail worn over a jerkin and fastened round the waist with a leather belt, a royal purple velvet cloak with gold lining fastened round the neck and hanging loosely from the shoulders, thigh-length black stockings, raw-hide sandals fastened with tan leather thongs which criss-cross over the insteps and all the way up to the thighs. A round silver shield on which is engraved a raven, a large silver-headed battle-axe and a dagger hung from the belt complete what is a very handsome and striking dress.

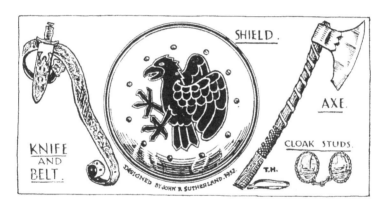

The imprint of a human foot and five toes as a Seal, while quite in keeping with the role of the leader in the revels, was scarcely suited to a Jarl's rank. After many suggestions it was finally decided to have a large red seal with a battle-axe engraved on it and bearing the motto 'We Axe for What We Want'.

Mr J. W. Robertson, who in after years became Convener of the County, had the honour of first wearing the Jarl's dress, and his appearance, standing on the poop of the long-ship, added a new dignity to the procession. Behind him marched over two hundred torch-bearing guizers, and the Docks Boys provided a beautiful replica in miniature of H.M.S. *Victory*. Before the Galleys received their last freight of blazing torches, the Guizers formed a circle round them and sang Burgess' new Up-Helly-Aa Song to the tune of "John Brown's Body".

Among the squads 'out' were—

Red Indians	Anglo-Saxons
Cake-walk Girls	Don Q
16th Century Peers	Judges
Dominoes	Father Christmas

The procession of 1907 was led by Mr J. H. Anderson as Guizer Jarl. His photograph in the new Jarl's dress was published in the Press. This established a practice which has been continued ever since. On the whole there was very little change from the arrangements for previous years. The want of a band to lead the Procession had long been felt. The strains of the fiddlers seated in the Galley could only be heard by those at close quarters, so this year two pipers were impressed to lead the Procession which they did with marked success. There was also an improvement in the lines of the Galley. Hitherto it has been customary to build the Galley from the water-line upwards, leaving the under-water portion to the imagination. This year it was built plank by plank right from the keel which gave the ship better lines and modified its previous dumpiness. Also another shield was added, making five on either side, but as yet the designers had not thought of adding oars.

The Docks Boys supplied a well-proportioned model of H.M.S. *Dreadnought,* which, in addition to her gun-turrets and armament, carried five boats slung in their davits and a smart steam pinnace complete in all details even to the propeller.

A visitor to Lerwick, who had witnessed the Up-Helly-Aa Festival for the first time, wrote a glowing account of all he had seen, but thought it was such a shame to see such fine models consumed by fire. He was, however, enthralled by the scene in the Rechabite Hall, which excelled any fancy-dress ball.

Among the squads 'out' were—

The Dam Family	Nursemaids
Firemen	Cowboys
Midshipmen	Clowns

1908 saw the first of the changes which finally resulted in the last Tuesday in January being fixed as the official date for the Festival, instead of the correct twentyfourth day after Yule, that is 29th January. The Guizers' Committee also persuaded the merchants to petition the Town Council to recommend that the day following Up-Helly-Aa should be a general holiday. In this they were successful, and a precedent was established which has continued ever since.

The Guizers' Committee also made another important decision. Each year it almost invariably happened that more than one squad would decide on the same dress. As it was a point of honour that dresses must be kept secret, it often happened that two or more squads would turn up more or less garbed in the same costume. To obviate this the Committee decided that, as soon as a squad fixed on their dress, they must intimate it to the secretary. In the event of a dress being duplicated, the first squad intimating it had priority of wearing it.

Mr W. Sinclair, who later became Provost of Lerwick, was Guizer Jarl. There was no change in the design of the Galley. The Docks Boys built a superb model of the *Great Harry*, having faithfully followed the design and colourings from a picture on a calendar. The model was twentyfour feet long and mounted no less than sixty guns. The *Great Harry* was put on show at the Market Cross during the day, and evoked great interest and many highly complimentary criticisms.

It did indeed seem a shame that such an artistic piece of work and craftsmanship should be destined so soon to make a bon-fire. One feels that the lines, said to have been engraved on a tomb-stone over an infant's grave, would have made a fitting epitaph to the *Great Harry*—

> "Since I have been so quickly done for,
> I wonder what I was begun for".

That epitaph, however, could, of course, be applied to all the Galleys.

Among the squads 'out' were—

Spanish Dancing Girls   Gollywogs
Kings and Queens   Gilbert Bain Nurses

The Kings and Queens had, as a dress, large playing cards depicting all the kings and queens in the pack. The Nurses were in hospital uniform. For some reason or other, they were out to poke fun at the grocers and bakers in the town who, in those days, were wont to send their Christmas greetings accompanied by a calendar, a bottle of wine and a currant loaf. The squad carried a banner emblazoned with the foregoing Christmas gifts and what appears to be a libellous statement on their qualities. It ran—

THE GREATEST DISCOVERY OF THE AGE.

KILL-EM QUICK. The Grand Cure for all Ills. Discovered by Drs Grocier and Bakier, and used in the Gilbert Bain Hospital.

Cures Sleeping Sickness, Socialism, Unemployment and the Drink Question.

An effective cure for the Dancing Craze (in proof of this, is largely used in Congregational Manses). One dose on Sunday will ensure a Pleasant Sunday Afternoon.

The subjects mentioned as amenable to the cure were all very much in the public eye at this time, and Pleasant Sunday Afternoons were the vogue.

More and more country folks were coming to the town to view or join in the festivities, and, unless they had friends who were entertaining the Guizers, they had nowhere to go after the procession was over. The Committee were very much concerned over this question, and made efforts to get the use of the drill-hall in the Fort, but the Royal Naval Reserve was occupying it, and, although very sympathetic, the authorities were unable to make it available, and the country cousins had to wait for another two years before they were catered for.

Before taking leave of 1908, mention must be made of a squad of four which went 'first fittin' on New Year's Eve. They were dressed up as old Shetland fishermen, with smookies (smocks) or reefer jackets, dungarees or well-patched moleskin trousers, sou'westers or Yaki caps, and all with rivlins on their feet. To put in time till midnight, the squad slowly traversed the Street as if they had just come in from the country and were determined to see what could be seen. Out of wrinkled old-men masks, adorned with the side or muffler type of whiskers, they gazed solemnly into the shop windows, pointing out to one another this or that article, and discussing its merits as compared with the things they had in their youth. Very soon they attracted the attention of the passers-by who crowded in to listen to their quaint old-fashioned conversation. Unlike the usual guizers, they paid no attention to any remarks addressed to them, but continued to wander from window to window, and by the time they had reached the end of the street they had a following which threatened to block the traffic.

Passing midnight they made their way to the home of Mr Robert Duthie, Chief Fishery Officer for Shetland. Mr Duthie's house was not one of the usual ports of call for guizers, so when Mrs Duthie answered the door, she was rather dubious about allowing them in. The 'old fishermen' protested that

L

they had tramped miles that day in order to confer with Mr Duthie, and they were not going home again until they did see him. They got their way, and Mr Duthie gave them a cordial welcome and asked what he could do for them. They did not leave him long in doubt. Complaint followed complaint about the depredations of the trawlers on the inshore grounds "til no sae muckle as a piltik or a haddock cood be got, an' whaat wis Maister Duthie gaen ta dae aboot it?" Then followed more complaints and long dissertations on the harm being done to the herring fishing by the killing of the whales. Mr Duthie must "ken hoo da fishermen depenit on de whaals to shew dem whaur de herrin' wis lying an' dis killin' o' de whaals wis coverin' de sea wi' sae muckle bluid dat a' da dogs i' de Atlaantic wis congregatin' on da herrin' grunds". The arguments became so serious and dogmatic, that Mr Duthie became quite oblivious to the fact that this was only a guizing 'aff-lay', and treated his guests to a spirited defence of the Scottish Fishery Board in what they had done to try to stop illegal trawling, and how they were constantly investigating the effects of whaling on the herring fishing. For a time he became quite heated as the 'fishermen' continued to reiterate their assertions that the Board was lacking in their efforts, and that they did not have the interests of the Shetland fishermen at heart. To tell the truth, the guizers, themselves, almost forgot that they were play-acting, and it was only a hint from one of the squad that there were other houses to visit, that brought the 'conference' to a close. The expression on Mr Duthie's face, when the guizers unmasked, was one of utter incredulity as he recognised four of his own friends. Even then he found it hard to get away from his defence of the Board, and to join in ordinary conversation, but the squad had had enough, and after a cup of tea and sandwiches they proceeded on their rounds.

The Committee published their Balance Sheet for 1908,

and it shews an expenditure of £28 14s. 4½d., which covered the cost of the Galley, Torches, Fireworks and Printing.

Still another future Provost of Lerwick, Mr James Laing, was elected Guizer Jarl for 1909, and his retinue consisted of twenty-two squads. The design of the Norse Galley was somewhat improved, and for the first time she carried, behind the dragon head, the pole with the blood-red hand on top; she was also equipped with ten shields on either side, and from beneath each shield an oar dipped into the sea. The Olna Whaling Company provided the Docks Boys with their choice of galley. As may have been gathered from the visit of the guizing squad to Mr Duthie, the whaling question was very much in evidence in local politics. The Docks Boys took for their model the whaling steamer *Arctic* and equipped her with harpoon gun and crow's nest. She carried the inscription "Caught within the 40 mile limit" and the slogan "Down with the Whalers".

In addition to a slight increase of houses 'open', the Town Hall, Rechabite Hall and Ganson's Hall were 'opened' by a number of hostesses, and the Queen's Hotel by the proprietor, so the guizers had an excellent night of enjoyment.

Of the more outstanding squads, there was a squad of Monkeys, with bells on their tails, who took full advantage of their simian character to gambol over everything, perch on window sills and mantelpieces, try with dire results to climb to the curtains in the Rechabite Hall, scratch and hunt for fleas, and generally to take licences that were denied to mere humans. The monkey-costumes were all hand-knitted from nigger-brown Shetland wool, and the masks of diverse monkey-faces, which blended so well into the suits, made the whole a marvellous disguise.

By way of contrast, the most charming, if such a description can be applied to a band of men masquerading in feminine array was the squad of Shepherdesses. They wore brightly-coloured sateen and cretonne costumes bedecked with many coloured ribbons after the style of the Dresden Shepherdess. Yes, 'charming' is the correct description.

Another squad which reflected the period was the Suffragettes, which characterisation gave them full play in holding forth in fervid harangues on the Rights of Women. The names on their visiting-cards were clever skits on the names of the ladies who were leaders of the movement—'Mrs Desperate' (Mrs Despard), 'Mrs Billious Greig' (Mrs Billington Greig) and 'Mrs Pathetic Lawrence' (Mrs Pethick Lawrence)—and the placards which adorned their figures, screeched aloud "Votes for We-men", "We demand our Rights" and "Justice ! Equality ! VOTES !"

There was also a squad who masqueraded as Dutch Girls. The costume was the typical Dutch dress with wooden clogs. The clogs were all right for clumping through the streets or clip-clopping in a dance, but after a time they became almost unbearable to feet which were unaccustomed to wearing them. The author was in this squad, and he well remembers splashing his way home at 6 a.m. through cold slushy mud *in his stocking soles.*

The adolescent period of Up-Helly-Aa was by now nearly over. A few more changes had to be tried out, but, on the whole, the lay-out and programme had become more or less standardised. The 1910 procession again consisted of twenty-two squads, and Mr G. T. Anderson presided over the festival as Guizer Jarl.

The Galley was built to the same model as in the previous year. The Docks Boys attained the highest pitch of their craftmanship in the designing and meticulous care with which they built a twenty-five-foot model of H.M.S. *St. Vincent.* The *St. Vincent* was photographed with the sea as background, and, in the resultant photograph which was reproduced in the Press, it is impossible without very minute scrutiny to believe that one is not looking at the real *St. Vincent* lying at anchor in the harbour. A further Galley took part in the procession, a Torpedo-boat Destroyer which was built on an old pulling gig. The long narrow lines of the gig were ideal for the purpose of modelling this type of vessel.

With fewer houses 'opening', the entertainment of the guizers was becoming more difficult. The additional 'opening' of the Grand Hotel eased the situation, but the plight of the country visitors, whose numbers were yearly increasing, was still a source of worry to the Committee. They had failed to get the drill hall in the Fort, and previous attempts to get the Territorial Drill Hall had also proved abortive. This year, however, they were at last successful in getting the Territorial Drill Hall, and it was reserved for country visitors only. Having secured the hall, the Committee recognised that, without refreshments or music, the hall could only be a place where the visitors could view the squads at close quarters, which would soon pall on a company which was itching to join in the dances. Arrangements were made with a baker to attend in the hall and provide pies, sandwiches, cakes, tea and soft drinks at moderate prices, and the services of a fiddler were engaged to assist the squad fiddlers or provide the music if any squad was without one. The venture was an immediate success in so far as the question of numbers was concerned. In fact, it was too much of a success, as the townspeople, who had nowhere else to go, crowded in and almost crowded out the visitors. The place was packed to suffocation, and the squads could scarcely squeeze their way in, much less carry out their programmes. In later years the Committee tried to remedy this state of affairs by issuing a limited number of tickets to genuine

country visitors, and appointing two door-keepers to ensure
that only ticket-holders were admitted.

Among the squads 'out' were—

Rosalind	Romeo
Grace Darling	Ally Sloper
Ghosts	Winter
Jack and the Bean-Stalk	Monkey Brand
Butchers	Old-Shetland Guizers

The Old-Shetland Guizers wore the 'gloy' or straw dress
which has already been fully described.

Mr E. S. Reid Tait, as Guizer Jarl, presided over the
Festival in 1911, and, so far as the weather was concerned,
he led the procession on what was probably the most glorious
night which up till then had ever favoured Up-Helly-Aa.
This year was the last occasion on which the Docks Boys
provided a galley for the procession. For some unknown reason
they deserted the British Navy, and took for their model the
U.S.A. battleship *North Dakota*. The British Navy was,
however, represented by a model of H.M.S. *Dido*, which was
built by a number of schoolboys. There was, too, an
innovation in the decoration of the Bill; instead of the usual
paintings across the top, the centre of the Bill was filled with
a well-done painting depicting a Viking in full battle-array.

Among the squads 'out' were—

Irish Paddies	Punch
Sir Walter Raleigh	Lord Nelson
Frogs	Fashions
Lerwick Cooking Class	Mad Hatters

"Fashions" was probably the most artistic squad, garbed in
all the variety and vagaries of the latest fashions. The
"Lerwick Cooking Class", with all sorts of cooking utensils

and materials, gave demonstrations of how to cook in ways that would be hard to find in any cookery book. A placard they carried declared that it was "Better to have cooked and killed than never to have cooked at all". The "Mad Hatters" from "Alice in Wonderland" were mad as mad could be, but, except for the dress, it is doubtful if Lewis Carrol would have recognised one of his most famous creations. They certainly caused the most amusement that night.

In 1912, Mr E. S. Reid Tait was again Guizer Jarl. Mr Harry Kay had been elected Jarl, but, owing to bereavement, he was unable to officiate. This was, indeed, a misfortune, as Mr Kay had been one of the most enthusiastic and hard-working members of the Committee. It is shrewdly suspected that he was also a very prominent member of the Jokes Committee.

For some years past, the Guizers' Committee had been gradually coming round to the view that modern battleships, however well-built, were not in keeping with the Viking spirit of the Festival. They, therefore, decided to ask the Docks Boys to build the Norse Galley, and after some negotiation, this they agreed to do. They gave their time and labour free, and it is on record that the cost of all the materials used in its construction amounted to £15 7s. The day of 'acquiring' all the necessary materials was indeed over. The Galley they built was thirty feet long, and the Dragon's Head stood thirteen feet above ground level.

Not only did the Docks Boys build the Galley, but they decided on a Viking dress for one of their squads. This squad did not draw first place in the Procession, but, when they made their appearance, and in view of the appropriateness of their dress, the Committee asked them to head the Procession as escort to the Galley. To the Docks Boys must, therefore, go the credit of being the originators of what later became an

established order, that the Guizer Jarl's squad must invariably
be dressed as Viking warriors and always head the Procession.
Among the squads 'out' were—

Weary Willie and Tired Tim	Peter Pan
Nancy Lee	Principal Boys
Ancient Mariners	Sisters of Mercy
Babies	Town Hall Tower and Bells

The "Babies" were all in prams wheeled by their respective
'mothers', and had all the paraphernalia of babyhood, feeding
bottles, soothing teats and articles which need not here be
described. Not only was their programme a 'scream' but they
were undoubtedly a screaming lot. The squad representing
Town Hall Tower and Bells were dressed in pink and green
costumes, and carried with them an excellently made replica of
the Tower with exact details of the architecture and the four clock
faces. Each member wore, as headgear, miniature models of
the Tower inside which were bells of varying tones. The
carillon they played would have shocked the makers of the
bells but added greatly to the fun.

Up-Helly-Aa 1913 was marred by bad weather. It
was so bad that it was out of the question to exhibit the Bill
at the Market Cross till through the forenoon, otherwise it
would have been ruined before the Public had a chance to
appreciate its rather clever contents. The plans and estimates
for the new Small Boat Harbour had been published, and, as
usual, there had been many divergent views on the selection
of the site and the costs. The Jokes Committee added their
comments to the discussion by painting, in the centre of the
Bill, the portrait of an old lady. She is seen gravely studying
the plans which she holds in her hands. In the harbour basin
enclosed by the proposed new breakwater, there stands out in
large bold figures "£40,000" : the old lady's comment is
"This is no joke" !

Mr McGowan Scott was elected Guizer Jarl, and was the first Jarl to command an Up-Helly-Aa Long-ship to which a name had been given. She was called *Thor* after that mighty Scandinavian god of Thunder. A new feature was tried out this year but it was not repeated. Before the torches were thrown into the Galley, the Guizer Jarl made a speech acclaiming Up-Helly-Aa and the traditions it carried with it. After the speech, he called for three cheers for the Festival, and then for three cheers for those who entertained the Guizers. The weather was certainly against speech-making, but it was more than evident that the Guizers were not enamoured with this innovation. They cheered for Up-Helly-Aa, but, when the Jarl called for cheers for their hosts and hostesses, the whole assembly gave a resounding response, and spontaneously broke into "For they are jolly good fellows". As stated, speech-making was not repeated, but each year thereafter hearty cheers have always been given for the Festival, the Hostesses, and, later on, for the Committee and the Guizer Jarl.

Another innovation, which was adopted and adhered to ever after, was a complete change in the route of the Procession. Up to this year it had always started from the Market Cross, but now the squads assembled on the South Hillhead at the top of Queen's Lane, and, after drawing torches, they were marshalled westwards in two lines set well apart. The Galley was brought from the Docks by an escort with torches and stationed in the rear of the formed-up Guizers. At the sound of a bugle-call, the torches were set alight, and the Galley with the Jarl on the poop, led by the Boy Scouts' Flute-and-Drum Band in front and the massed fiddlers behind, passed majestically through the lines of torch-bearers to take up its position in the van. The Procession then made its way through the Lower Hillhead, King Erik Street, King Harald Street, Harbour Street, St. Olaf Street, Commercial Road and so on

to the Market Cross, where the 'burning' took place.   In later
years Harbour Street and St. Olaf Street were cut out.   The
new route was much superior to the old one as it allowed the
spectators better coigns of vantage from which to view the
Procession, and the old danger of sticking in Queen's Lane was
avoided.   In this connection it may be mentioned that on one
occasion, the Galley was made a fraction too wide, and did
stick in the narrowest part of Queen's Lane, much to the
amusement of the spectators and the ire of the Guizers.

Among the twenty-two squads 'out' were—

Billiards	Little Tich
Wilkin Micawber	French Clowns
Lloyd George	Bubbles
Fry's Five Chocolate Boys	Faust
Mercutio	Which is the Better Half?

The last named squad wore a clever dress.   One side of the
costume was made up in uniform black gentleman's suits, while
the other side sported the latest dress fashions for ladies.   The
masks conformed to the dress, one side of the face adorned
with an elegant moustache, while the other portrayed various
types of feminine beauty.

There was no change in the programme for Up-Helly-Aa
in 1914.   Mr Laurence Sandison was Guizer Jarl.   He had a
magnificent Galley, which was built to the design of the
Gokstad Viking Ship which had been discovered in Norway
in 1880.   Little did the builders of the Gokstad Ship dream
that more than a thousand years later their masterpiece would
serve as a "model" for a Long-ship in a Lerwick Up-Helly-
Aa procession, or that the eyes in the dragon head would send
forth gleaming rays of light—a very modern touch achieved
by the use of electric flashlights.   The festival Long-ship was

named *Aegers Hest,* which was painted in runic characters on the stern. The name was taken from the Norse lore, Aeger being the goddess of the sea, and Hest, a horse. The 'Coming of Age' of Up-Helly-Aa was now indeed accomplished, and, as if to celebrate the event, a mere mundane harbour contractor was called upon to add more glory to the scene. The building of the new harbour works had commenced, and the contractors, Kinnear, Moodie & Co., had an electric cable running from the harbour to their quarries at the Knab. They tapped the cable at the top of Queen's Lane, and provided flood-lighting for the muster of the Guizers, a thoughtful gesture on the part of strangers which was very much appreciated.

A finishing touch was given to the Procession by the provision of Brass and Fife Bands totalling twenty-four instrumentalists who had been specially trained by ex-Guizer Jarl McGowan Scott and Mr William Grant respectively.

The entertainment of the Guizers was now mainly in the hands of various groups of ladies and gentlemen who engaged the halls or hotels. Only four private houses were 'opened', but the Town, Rechabite, Good Templars', and Territorial Halls together with the Grand and Queen's hotels provided ample accommodation, refreshment and young ladies to ensure all a very happy enjoyable night.

Among the twenty-two squads 'out' were—

The Saftest o' the Faimily.	Prehistoric Man
Dressmakers	Evening Dress 1960
Strayed Parcels	Crimson Ramblers
The Lerwick Corporation	Stars and Stripes
Cleansing Department	Britannia

It is almost unnecessary to describe the dress worn by the "Cleansing Department". Each member of the squad took upon himself the task of studying and impersonating one of the members of the staff, and their masks were unmistakable life-like caricatures of their originals. The best likeness was that of the Burgh Chief Constable who was also head of the Department. The squad had all the paraphernalia of their profession—barrows, brooms, shovels, etc., and on their entry they made a great display of their craft under the direction of the Chief. They even managed to mimic the voices and idiosyncrasies of their 'doubles' which their audience was not slow to recognise, a feature which added enormously to the effectiveness of this masquerade.

Little has been said about the juveniles, but they were by no means out of the picture on Up-Helly-Aa night. As of old they still tried to copy the 'older boys', and had their own galleys, torches and processions which took place in the earlier part of the evening. They were usually assisted by old-time guizers who took the fullest pleasure in dressing their young hopefuls in full Viking Jarl's dress, and in building their galleys, many of which were beautiful miniatures of the Galley.

So ended the last Up-Helly-Aa Festival before the First World War, which called away the youth of the town to sterner tasks, from which many of the brightest guizers failed to return.

CHAPTER XIX.

MANHOOD.

WHEN the war, which people fondly hoped was to end wars, was over, the youth of Lerwick turned their thoughts once more to the revival of the Yule festivities, but more especially to the celebration of Up-Helly-Aa. Five Up-Helly-Aas had passed, celebrated only by some Squad suppers and dances. The younger generation was eager to make up for lost time, and there were plenty of the younger old-stagers ready to co-operate, while many of the older old-stagers retired from the fray, and assumed the role of hosts.

The first post-war Up-Helly-Aa was celebrated on 27th January, 1920. The weather was most unpropitious; it was blowing a gale and the rain was coming down in torrents; so bad was it that the start of the procession was postponed for a couple of hours, by which time the rain had ceased, but with the wind still howling the torches would have been burned out long ere the procession was over, so the route was shortened.

During the inter-war years the Up-Helly-Aa festivities were all more or less of a pattern : the child had grown into a man, and, after the manner of its human counterpart, it settled down to that even tenor of its way which, while revelling in the fulness of life, resents being upset by radical changes in its mode of living. It would, therefore, be wearisome to make a chronological survey of each Up-Helly-Aa with its Guizer Jarl, its Galley and its Squads; those interested in data referring to the inter-war years will find these tabulated on a later page. We shall, therefore, deal with items of interest, a few descriptions of the more outstanding squads and such changes of procedure as were introduced during these years.

It has already been noted that in 1912 the Docks Boys had provided a squad of Vikings who were asked to escort the Galley in the procession. In 1921 the Guizers' Committee decided that this feature should become an integral part of the procession, and that the Guizer Jarl should wear his Jarl's dress throughout the night. Up to the date of this decision it had been customary for the Jarl to doff his official dress and don the dress of his own particular squad.

The decision to have a Viking Squad each year resulted in the production of some of the finest dresses ever seen on Up-Helly-Aa or, indeed, at any fancy-dress ball. Mostly the Viking Squads chose for their models Norse gods or heroes— Olaf Tryggvason (king of Norway circa 980), Frithiof (famous mythological Norse hero), Frey (god of summer), Njord (god of Wealth, Sea and Fire), Ullr (god of Archery and Winter), Varanger Guard (the personal bodyguard of a Greek empress of Constantinople) and Hjaltlanders, to mention a few. A detailed description of two of these dresses will indicate the meticulous care and trouble that the Guizer Jarl's squad took to make them look the part. Portrayal of the gods gave reign to imagination and skill.

Take Njord and note how the design of the dress was emblematic of his dominion over Wealth, Sea and Fire. From the shoulders hung a flowing red cloak lined inside with royal blue, and edged with gold. Under the cloak was a red tunic adorned with masses of scintillating gold and silver sequins, re-producing in a wonderful manner the glittering phosphorescent sheen or 'mareel' so often seen on an autumn sea. The legs were clad in red skintights cross-gartered in blue and white, while the feet were encased in rivlins profusely covered with seaweed. The god's long flaxen hair was only partially obscured by his helmet which was surmounted by the head of a serpent flanked by two golden wings. The shield had an outline of a serpent running round the outer edge, while on the centre was an artistic painting of the Dore Holm with two whales swimming on the surface of a placid sea.

The second description is of another Norse god, Ullr, the god of Archery and Winter. The mantle was light blue-slate lined with white, trimmed with white fur. The short-sleeved tunic was green and edged with white fur. The leg skintights were red, cross-gartered in yellow, and the foot-gear was made from undressed hide. From the black leather belt, fastened with a heavy metal buckle and embellished with brass ornaments, hung a sword with rope-bound studded hand-grip and black hand-guard. The helmet, bearing a gold crest, was green and was adorned with wings made from handsome white black-tipped feathers, and displayed on the front was a diamond of white metal and brass. Round the forehead was a circlet of white metal cut in the shape of skates, which *Ullr* was wont to use for his winter journeyings, while over his shoulder was slung a hunting-horn. The hair, as in all Norse characterisations, was flaxen. The most artistic part of the *tout ensemble* was the silver shield, which bore a painting of the Ward of Bressay covered with a coating of snow glistening under a fine display of the Northern Lights, and, as if to balance the vivid painting of the Aurora, the bottom of the shield was decorated with a green bow with crossed arrows tipped with gold.

Both these dresses richly merited the description 'gorgeous'.

The Viking dresses, other than those whose inspiration was drawn from Norse mythology, mainly followed the lines of the Guizer Jarl's costume, to which occasionally was added a dressed white sheepskin worn over the back—a very comfortable adjunct on a cold night, but, in the heated atmosphere of the dance, well ! not so good.

Beyond a few minor changes here and there, according to the ideas of the builders, the Galleys continued to be made to the lines and plans of former models ; in fact, it is difficult to visualise what further embellishments could be made to this heraldic dragon-ship. The admirable practice of giving names to the Galleys was now definitely established, and, of the twenty long-ships built during the inter-war years, only the first two were nameless. Here again Norse mythology and history were drawn upon to supply names which were not only saturated with the tang of the North, but which also whetted one's desire to know more of the lore which produced them—Ormr (serpent), Sae-Orn (sea eagle), Odur (personification of the sun), Frithr (peace) and Jola-Tungl (Yule Moon).

The only marked change in the torchlight procession was the introduction, in 1921, of the Turning Movement which was first carried out on the Town Hall Brae (King Erik Street). For a time the Town Hall Brae, with its wide open roadway providing plenty of space for the spectators, was an ideal position, but, as the number of the guizers increased, the Brae became too congested to allow the Movement to be shewn to advantage, and the site for the Turning Movement was transferred to King Harald Street. Here, at a selected point, the Galley is halted, and the two lines of torch-bearers swing outwards and countermarch until they join up with the tail of the procession, and again form two lines. To the blare of the Town Brass Band and the skirl of the bagpipes of the British Legion Pipe Band, the four lines of torches lighting up the multicoloured, fascinating, fantastic, weird and gorgeous dresses and masks of the guizers, marching and countermarching under a thick cloud of lurid smoke, create a scene which can never be forgotten, and when, as in 1938, the Turning Movement was carried out under a magnificent and almost terrifying blood-red Aurora Borealis, the scene beggars description. The military precision with which the Movement is enacted is entirely due to the indefatigable supervision of the Committee Men who take control of the procession from start to finish.

There was one small change introduced in 1934. When the Galley arrived at its appointed place, the Guizer Jarl's squad slowly circled round it as the remainder of the procession took up position to perform the 'last rites'. With the Jarl, in full battle array, standing on the quarter-deck, and the Viking warriors slowly marching round the doomed ship, an impressive scene is created which adds greatly to the symbolism of the pageant. Only one more touch is required to make the final obsequies complete, and that is for the Guizer Jarl to assume a recumbent position on a bier amidships before his warriors take farewell of him, but the frailty of human nature cannot be trusted, and Guizer Jarls are not likely to feign death and risk being the target for a blazing torch directed by some irrepressible humorist.

In 1935 the Guizers acquired yet another song, and it came about in this way. A good many years ago, Mr John Nicolson, author of "Tales of Thule", etc., dedicated to Norway a short poem which he called "Northland Skaal" ("Hail Northland") which dwelt on the ties which bound Shetland and Norway. This poem was translated into Norwegian and set to a stirring tune adapted from an old Norwegian folk-song. Some enthusiastic guizers wanted to adopt "Northland Skaal" as an Up-Helly-Aa song, but, after consideration, it was decided that the words and sentiments of the original poem were not just

M

suitable for the occasion. Mr Nicolson agreed with this decision, and wrote another song which he named "The Galley Song", and which is sung to the air of "Northland Skaal".

THE GALLEY SONG.

Floats the raven banner o'er us,
 Round our Dragon Ship we stand,
Voices joined in gladsome chorus,
 Raised aloft the flaming brand.

Every guizer has his duty
 When he joins the festive throng:
Honour freedom. love and beauty
 In the feast, the dance, the song.

Worthy sons of Vikings make us,
 Truth be our encircling fire;
Shadowy visions backward take us
 To the Sea-king's fun'ral pyre.

Bonds of Brotherhood inherit,
 O'er strife the curtain draw;
Let our actions breathe the spirit
 Of our grand Up-Helli-Aa.

The Guizers now have three songs :—The Up-Helly-Aa Song which is sung as the procession moves off, The Galley Song which precedes the throwing-in of the torches, and The Norseman's Home which is sung after the Galley is well ablaze. To ensure that the Guizers know the words and tunes of their songs, the Brass Band attends the mass meeting of the guizers each year, when the songs are practised.

The claims of the Gilbert Bain Memorial Hospital were brought to the notice of the Guizers' Committee. In 1920 they staged a fancy-dress football match on the day following the festival, but it was not till 1925 that a serious effort was made to raise funds. This they did by organising a daylight procession of all the guizers on the afternoon following Up-Helly-Aa, and this procession is now an annual event. The guizers enter whole-heartedly into the task of extracting skat from the Honourable Burgesses. The squads march in formation while two members from each harry the sightseers with pocks, pails, tin baths, kishies and even a bed-sheet carried stretched by four vociferous beggars. Also helping in this good cause can be seen the individual guizer or a New'r's Eve squad whose 'aff-lay' and antics materially help to fill the coffers.

In 1926 H.M.S. *Harebell* put into Lerwick harbour, and, as soon as the ship's company realised that their arrival had coincided with Up-Helly-Aa, there was a general request to be allowed to join in the revels. The Guizers felt that to accede to this wholesale petition would not be practicable, but they did grant permission for two squads of sailors to take part, and arranged for the shore-leave officers and ratings to be allocated to various places of entertainment. If Jack Tar was not altogether *au fait* with the art of squad uniformity of dress, he certainly made the best of what he could lay his hands on, and entered into the spirit of the festival with a zest that captivated his hosts.

Reference has previously been made to the high standard of artistic skill which was lavished on the decoration of the Bill. Perhaps the most artistic was the Bill of 1933, the work of Mr Tom Henry. In that year the Guizer Jarl's squad represented the famous mythological Norse hero Frithiof, and this inspired Mr Henry to devote the decoration of the Bill solely to scenes from the Frithiof Saga. Across the top was a vigorous fjord scene with Frithiof as the central figure directing the loading of booty by the Vikings into long-ships, while around the margin of the Bill were eleven scenes depicting episodes in Frithiof's life as narrated in the saga. Fortunately the custom of photographing the Bill had been in vogue for a number of years, so that we can still admire a masterpiece which like the beautiful Passion Flower blooms for a day and is gone.

It had long been felt that no year-to-year photographic records of Up-Helly-Aa were being kept. Individuals had hundreds of photographs stowed away in boxes and albums, but usually these were of interest only to the persons concerned. To remedy this the Committee decided, in 1922, that an official album should be kept by the Secretary into which would be mounted annually photographs of the Committee, Guizer Jarl, Collecting Sheet, The Bill and all the squad photographs. They, further, decided that copies of all Newspaper Reports should be preserved in an album deposited for safe custody in the care of the curator of the News Room. It was in that same year that the first printed programme giving the text of the Collecting Sheet, the Bill, Songs etc., appeared. In later years a photograph of the Guizer Jarl appeared on the front page.

It was inevitable that the spectacular nature of the Up-Helly-Aa Festival would, sooner or later, attract the attention of the cinematographers. In 1926, the Gaumont Graphic Company sent a representative to Lerwick who filmed the procession and the bonfire, and, on the following day, he persuaded the Guizer Jarl's squad, Helgeland Vikings, to be filmed at the Slates Pier. The following year the same Company filmed the Jarl's squad, Olaf Tryggvason, aboard their Long-ship *Ormr*. That year, too, the squad of Walruses was filmed, crawling and posturing among the rocks at Sound. Since then, other film companies have sent their operators to take 'shots' of the Festival. The local photographers, too, have regularly taken some very excellent 'stills' of the procession and bonfire.

In 1927, J. J. Haldane Burgess, blind poet and author,

died, and the Guizers lost their chief friend and adviser. It is principally to Haldane Burgess that we owe Up-Helly-Aa as we now know it. The late William Sinclair, for many years one of the most enthusiastic members of the Committee, told the writer that, before attending a Guizers' Meeting, he invariably called on Haldane Burgess for his advice and suggestions. "In fact", he said, "I was Burgess' mouthpiece, and if his advice and suggestions could be carried out, they were invariably adopted". To him the Guizers owe the heraldic galley, the change from The Worthy Chief Guizer to Guizer Jarl, the details for Viking dresses, and the Up-Helly-Aa Song.

From 1933 onwards the Docks Boys ceased to have separate representation on the Guizers' Committee, and were, thereafter, elected along with others when vacancies had to be filled.

The foregoing, then, are the principal changes in the inter-war years; no change, indeed, but rather a mere polishing-up of a set piece.

The squads were as varied as ever, but there was an increase in what may be called 'mixed group guizing'. One of these group squads maintained a "Tirvil" tradition for, at least, four consecutive years : Tirvil's Waddin', Tirvil's Bairns, Tirvil's Cairdin', and Tirvil's Circus. The first of these, Tirvil's Waddin', was undoubtedly the best, and they staged an old-fashioned Shetland wedding, re-enacting every phase of the ceremony[55]. The first of the squad to enter the hall was the old-time Gunman, who let off some bangs. He was followed by two Fiddlers who preceded the Bride and the

---

[55]The usual order of a bridal procession to the church was—Gunman, fiddlers, the married or 'honest' pair (not necessarily husband and wife), the bride and the best man, the best maid and the bridegroom, after whom followed the guests in pairs. On leaving the church, the only change was that the bride and bridegroom paired, as, also, did the best man and best maid.

Bridegroom; next came the Best Man and Best Maid, then the Minister followed by the Married Pair, and behind them, the Guests all marching two and two. No wedding is complete without a Bridescake, and the one, supplied for this wedding, must have been the last word in bridescakes, but what is more remarkable it walked in. It was an excellent replica of a tiered wedding-cake, was seven feet in height, and enveloped the form of a stalwart guizer. The whole squad were dressed in the fashions of their grandparents, and it was hard to believe that not one of the 'ladies' belonged to the fair sex. The Bride was all that a bride should be, dainty and somewhat coy. The wedding ceremony was carried through, and, thereafter, the whole company danced a Shetland reel, finishing up with the traditional rite of 'Kissin' da lasses'.

There were twenty-three in this squad, and it had in its ranks a good many 'old-timers', including, at least, two former Jarls and one Worthy Chief. A local statistician computed the squad's combined ages at 1035 years, which made their average 45. Youth will have its day!

The following is a selection of 'topical' group squads :—

In 1927, the Sheepdog Trials squad carried through a very humorous act, suggested by sheepdog trials which had taken place in the previous year. There were two Judges, two Shepherds, two Dogs and five Sheep. A wooden pen was set up into which the 'dogs' had to drive the 'sheep'. Never were there such recalcitrant sheep; the dogs barked, the shepherds blew their whistles and went through the whole pantomime of working their dogs while the judges took notes and finally gave their somewhat amusing verdicts.

In 1929, a squad paraded under the name of "The 'Male' She Left Behind Her", which title completely misled everyone until the actual play-acting began. It was a skit on a lapse by the Post Office which inadvertently delivered the Lerwick mails from the mail steamer *St. Ninian* at Kirkwall. The incident caused a good deal of 'heat' at the time. There were twelve guizers in the squad, ten of whom were totally enclosed in mail-bags, stencilled back and front ABERDEEN TO LERWICK. Only the arms were free, and they were adorned with envelopes with highly humorous topical addresses on them. The bags were tied round the necks of the 'contents'; the protruding tops formed the head-dresses. The remaining two of the squad were dressed in well-worn dusty dungarees with masks which portrayed the physiognomies of two well-known storemen. The storemen wheeled in on their barrows two or three bags at a time, nonchalantly dumped them on to the floor, and went out for more until the whole ten lay in a heap. The groans and muttered imprecations which came from the heap signified that the lowermost 'bags' were far from happy. In due course the 'mails' were tipped out, and, in spite of their dishevelment, forthwith proceeded to deliver letters, the subtle addressing of which must have taxed the wit of the squad and afforded them many a hearty laugh. Inside each envelope was the squad's song, a skit on the 'missing mail' incident. To give further point to their ploy, they took round with them a four-foot model of the *St. Ninian.*

Still another group squad was "The Charge of the Soond Brigade", which took for its subject the varied milk-sellers who daily delivered their milk in Lerwick from Sound. The members must have devoted a considerable time to studying the dresses, mannerisms and voices of their originals. Leading the squad was a miniature motor milk van, complete with pails, and bearing the legend 'The Charge of the Soond Brigade, 3d. a Pint". Then followed a group of old wives and old men, mostly wearing rivlins, and young ones in sand-shoes, some carrying kishies with pails in their hands, others with pails and baskets, one with a converted pram, and another with a box mounted on an ancient pram chassis, and all with strikingly life-like masks. As the milk-sellers wandered round the guests, appraising the excellent quality of their milk, a well known local 'policeman' accosted each in turn and took samples of the milk, which he solemnly tested, or rather tasted, until he came on one which he decided did not contain the requisite amount of butter-fat, arrested the alleged delinquent and marched her off. Although the victims of this skit may not have relished being impersonated, the squad were careful not to give undue cause for offence.

It may be here mentioned that most of the lifelike *papier maché* masks of the foregoing and other topical squads, were made by Mr Arthur Abernethy, the artist who embellished the Collecting Sheets. Mr Abernethy also made the masks for

the squads 'out' as "Alice in Wonderland", "Snow White And The Seven Dwarfs" and other characters. In 1930, he made masks for no less than eight squads. It may be added that he made his first masks in 1920, in response to the imaginative importunity of a squad of schoolboys and other youths, who chose the *Daily Mail* war-time cartoon character Dilly-Dally. Another mask-maker was Mr John Smith, painter, Lerwick.

During the inter-war years, too, there was an increase in animal presentations, and even a fish provided one squad with model for a dress. In 1921, we had the ''Snulligarth Zoological Gardens'' which toured the halls with dogs, cats, bears, leopards and so on, not forgetting a pigmy elephant, which dress very effectively hid two hefty guizers.

In the early Twenties Pogo was all the craze so it was inevitable that it should claim a place in the Up-Helly-Aa festival. It was a much too strenuous form of amusement, and had a very short life. In order to understand what follows, a brief description of this game is necessary. Pogo sticks were like broom handles with a crosspiece resting on a powerful spiral spring some distance from the foot. The performer clasped the top of the stick and stepped on to the crosspiece with both feet, and immediately commenced to hop. A considerable amount of practice was necessary to attain proficiency, and the squad who went 'out' as Pogo Fiends put in a good deal before Up-Helly-Aa. One evening they met for practice in the house of one member of the squad whose wife was out for the evening. Quite unperturbed about the damage they were inflicting on the carpet, they were hopping about with varying degrees of success when the door opened and in came a late member who apparently had been putting in some practice on his own. He announced that 'he had fairly got the trick of it now', and to show that this was no vain boast he mounted his stick and commenced to hop. Now, until one has mastered the art of Pogo-hopping, each successive hop is higher and longer than the preceding one. Our 'expert' controlled the first hop or two and then the stick took charge. Across the room he went in ever increasing bounds, the final one of which projected him through the bay window on to the flower bed outside. Half of this squad was dressed in Fair Isle jerseys and skirts, the other half as schoolboys in schoolboy clothes. They created no small sensation and even some trepidation among the guests as they hopped uncertainly into the halls.

One of the most splendid of the animal squads was "Chanticleer", who strutted around completely feathered from head to foot, some in white and others in brilliantly-hued feathers. The arms manipulated wings, and the magnificent tails swept upwards and downwards in graceful curves. The realistic cocks' heads were also fully feathered, each with a brilliant red comb, yellow beak and piercing eyes—another instance of Mr Abernethy's skill as a maskmaker. The legs were yellow, and the feet were adorned with huge claws which were kept constantly in use scratching the ground or skilfully allaying some irritating itch. As some fine black and white ostrich feathers were incorporated in the dress, it is safe to assume that they had been 'acquired' from mother's or grannie's wardrobe. As might be expected their 'signature tune' was 'Cock-a-doodle-doo', which varied in tone and strength from almost a love-lilt to a strident cracked screech. An old woman, with a cog of corn, tended the Chanticleers—"tuck, tuck, tucking" as she scattered the grain on the ground.

Another 'bird' squad was "The Night Birds", who were dressed in a very fine imitation of tawny owls. The dress was made of heavy tawny velvet with wired-on-wings, talons on the feet, and excellent owl's-head masks. The latter with their saucerlike eyes and curved beaks, presented learned judge-like expressions which hid, in this squad, the Sheriff and at least one member of the Bar.

Before leaving the 'bird' squads, mention must be made of *Aptenodytes Pennanti*. This awe-inspiring name on the programme completely puzzled everyone until a squad of penguins waddled their stately way into the halls. After due interrogation, it was discovered that, with a keen sense of humour, the squad had hidden their identity by the use of the Latin name for a well-known Antarctic penguin. The dress fully justified the ingenuity the squad exercised in naming it.

In 1926, a rather unusual visitor paid a call on the Shetland Isles. It was a Walrus, and, as may be imagined, its appearance was not lost on the guizers, ever on the outlook for new ideas for Up-Helly-Aa dresses. No fewer than nine squads intimated to the Secretary that they were going 'out' as Walruses. In accordance with the Committee's rules, the first squad intimating their choice, when more than one squad had chosen the same subject, had the preference, and they called themselves Shetland's Mysterious Visitor. Surely this was the hottest dress ever worn at Up-Helly-Aa ; the imitation fur cloth had to be all padded out until the natural rotundity of the Walrus was obtained. The designers had faithfully copied the flippers and claws, while the whiskered head, with its tusks and big round eyes, was particularly realistic. As the herd crawled and flapped their way into the places of entertainment, they presented one of the most amusing and, incidentally, one of the most striking entries ever made by any squad at Up-Helly-Aa. As already noted this squad was filmed on the rocks at Sound.

Another visitation to Shetland waters, but this time by no means welcome, provided the subject for a dress. In 1930, there had been large numbers of cuttle-fish on the herring grounds, which, attacking the herring in the nets, rendered large quantities of them useless. In Shetland, the local name for the cuttle-fish is 'skeetick', and as "Da Skeeticks", did one squad go 'out' on the following Up-Helly-Aa. The dress was a very good imitation of the 'skeetick', but the head, with its mass of octopus-like tentacles and stony staring eyes, gave one the creeps. "Da Skeeticks" were accompanied by two fishermen, dressed in smocks and sea-boots, carrying nets in which were a few partially destroyed herrings which provided the theme for a mournful 'aff-lay' on the losses they had sustained through 'dis plague o' skeeticks'.

A fantasy and a fairy-tale were responsible for two of the most gorgeously dressed squads which ever brightened the revels of the Festival.

In 1934, a squad masqueraded as "Alice in Wonderland". All the characters in the fantasy were there—Alice, the Dormouse, the White Rabbit, the Mad Hatter, the Caterpillar, the Fish Footman and the Lobster, the Ugly Duchess and the Cook, the King and Queen, Tweedledum and Tweedledee, and the White Knight. The dresses and masks were made locally, and were wonderful replicas of Tenniel's drawings. It was evident that the various characters had made a study of Lewis Carrol's famous book, which was reflected in their 'aff-lay', but the main attraction was the *tout ensemble* of the squad.

The squad which in 1939 took a fairy tale for their motif, chose "Snow White and the Seven Dwarfs" as depicted in Walt Disney's well-known technicolor film, and permission to portray the characters had to be obtained from Walt Disney Mickey Mouse Ltd. First to enter the halls was a compère splendidly dressed in red and black evening suit. With an easy flowing descriptive speech, he introduced the characters as they paraded in, first, Snow White in a charming blue and white dress, followed by Prince Charming, the Queen, the Huntsman and the Witch, all in gorgeous attire. After these were introduced, in turn, the famous Seven Dwarfs, Doc, Grumpy, Happy, Sneezy, Bashful, Sleepy and Dopey, arrayed in gnome costumes in red, brown, green, blue and yellow. Last of all lopped in Five Rabbits in close-fitting furry dresses. We have frequently remarked on the masks fashioned by Mr

Abernethy, but those made for the Seven Dwarfs, were masterpieces which portrayed the varying characterisations of each with extraordinary skill. It is almost needless to say that the Dwarfs' song "Heigho ! Heigho ! Off to Work We Go" constituted one of the features of the play-acting.

In 1938 a squad of sixteen, excluding the fiddler and his acolyte, portrayed sixteen of the principal figures in the Gilbert and Sullivan operas. The brilliant uniforms and colourful dresses blended marvellously with the more sombre attire of the legal profession and its satellites, the Executioner and the Policeman, and made the Savoyards closely rival the magnificence of that other outstanding squad of this same year, the Hjaltlanders. Quite a number of the squad had taken part in the presentations of the operas in Lerwick, so it was only natural that hosts and guests should be entertained to snatches of the songs as each character introduced himself. In one corner of the room could be heard a voice intimating that the owner thereof was "a right good judge" while next to him another declaimed that he was "ruler of the Queen's Navee". From another part of the room a stentorian voice proclaimed "I am the Pirate King", and seemed quite uninterested in his neighbour who was insisting that he was a "Major General". It is interesting to note that the Savoyards had in their ranks the Member of Parliament for the County, an ex-Convener of the County who later became Provost of Lerwick, the Vice-Convener, destined to become Convener, and the Sheriff. Truly might the shades of the tar-barrellers come forth and stare with unbelieving eyes !

During the inter-war years, no fewer than 597 squads took part in the festival, and, as it is the unwritten law that no dress which has been 'out' on one Up-Helly-Aa shall appear at another, it makes one marvel at the fertile brains which evolve fresh characterisations and dresses year after year. Time was when the guizers designed and made their own guizing dresses, but nowadays, speaking generally, a guizing dress, designed and made by the wearer, could well have been included as an exhibit by the squad who 'went out' as Things Of The Past. For many years now, the guizers have depended on the local dressmakers who have served them well, and have gone to no end of trouble to make the guizers look their parts. The cost of the dresses, too, has increased as the squads have gone in for more elaborate designs, but even in 1939 one could still see a costume which did not cost the wearer more than a few shillings, while at the other end of the scale there have been dresses costing over £7. It has been computed that the average cost of the modern Up-Helly-Aa dress was between £4 and £5. Of late years, too, some of the squads have hired their dresses from London costumiers, but this practice is usually only indulged in when all the members of the squad represent different characters, such as in The Savoyards.

Details of only a few squads have been given, but these must be taken as only samples of the more outstanding ones. Each Guizer Jarl's squad deserves special description, but so, also, would Alladin, The Merry Milkmaids, The Killjoys, whose slogans all began with 'Thou shalt not'; Big Aggie's Man, whose dress and mask were the same back and front; Mutt and Jeff, The Scarlet Fever Microbes, fearsome to look upon; Old Bill, with his famous moustache; That Kruschen Feeling, which gave the squad such elated spirits; Bobbed, the headless knight; The Toy Drum Major; The Broch Lodgers, denizens of the Pictish castles; Awful Tired, who certainly looked it; The Three Arts, Music, Painting and Literature; Onion Johnnie, whose appearance revived happy memories (but where did they get the onions?); The Northern Diver, which was not a bird but a diver in diving dress; Miss 1928—Bachelors Beware, The Man In The Moon, Mr Yang

Kwen San, in beautiful silk Chinese dresses; The New Filters, which featured the Town's new plant; Up-Helly-Aa Clippings, in dresses made from the clippings left over from other Up-Helly-Aa dresses (a very colourful squad); Chimpie's Night Out, a monkey feature; Ghandi (a perfect mask, but a cold dress for a winter night); Hitler's Storm Troops, all swastikas and Nazi salutes; Things of the Past— stap, crappin, fourpence-a-gill, the schocner *Matchless* and a 'dreeler' of 1900; Priests of the Incas, an impressive, gorgeous dress; the Fish Brigade, skit on the local fish-vendors with their fish and chip van, barrows and baskets; Islenskir Fornbuningar, in their old-time Icelandic national dress; Town Litter, with their life-like masks and ashbins full of debris—one of the hits of the evening—and The Skeklers, in their old-Shetland straw dresses, to name a number taken at random.

CHAPTER XX.

THE FESTIVAL.

THIS narrative is drawing to a close, and to many, who have never been privileged to witness Up-Helly-Aa, a short account of the Festival as it is now will enable them to join with us in spirit when next the Guizer Jarl takes his stand on the poop of his Dragon-ship.

We have already spent the night and early morning with the Jokes Committee preparing the Bill, and it has now at last been securely fixed to the Pillar at the Market Cross. It is very dark as we make our way home to bed but the air is crisp and still giving promise of a fine quiet day. Some hours have yet to pass before the first rays of light appear away down on the south-eastern horizon, but, as soon as there is enough light to see, passers-by gather in front of the Bill to admire its artistic decoration but more especially to see who is 'in the Bill' and why. A chuckle or loud guffaw indicates that a shaft of wit has found its mark whether the target be some erring citizen, pompous councillor or local character. The lieges love to see the searchlight of wit, ridicule or castigation directed on the Affairs of State of the Capital and County of Thule, and thoroughly enjoy the quips and sallies aimed at the ongoings at kirk and market throughout the preceding year.

About 9.30 a.m. the Galley is taken from the shed in which it was built and is hauled down to the north end of the Fish Market where, for the remainder of the day, it will evoke the admiration of the crowds who come to gaze on its fine lines and its wonderful head and tail. During the day the Guizer Jarl and his squad of Vikings will visit the Galley, and have their photographs taken both aboard and standing by their Long-ship. At 7 p.m. the towropes are once more manned by a crowd of youngsters, and, escorted by torchbearers, the Galley makes its way to the South Hillhead where it will take station near the Big Kirk to await the arrival of the squads. By 8 o'clock the squads begin to arrive, and after being checked by the Committee Men, they draw their torches and are marshalled in two long lines westwards from the Galley. Soon all the squads have been accounted for and stand facing inwards with their torches held ready for lighting up, while at regular intervals between the lines, holding phosphorous flares or Roman candles, stand the Committee Men ready to perform this service.

Now, from the westward comes the sound of a Brass or Pipe Band, and the waiting lines of guizers stiffen to attention as the Guizer Jarl, at the head of his warriors, approaches and leads them smartly between the ranks till he halts them alongside the Galley. The Bands take up their respective positions, the Guizer Jarl climbs on to the poop of his Long-ship, and his warriors line up on either side as escort. A bugle sounds, and the Committee Men deftly light the torches from their flares, and in less than three minutes the whole South Hillhead from the Big Kirk to the top of Gullet's Brae is transformed from a sombre shadowy scene to a mellowed brilliance which reveals a riot of kaleidoscopic colour. The Marshal gives the order to march, the Band strikes up the Up-Helly-Aa Song, and the guizers lustily join in. They

N

may not all know the verses but they do know the chorus, and
it is with full-throated 'A-oi !' they answer the wild Viking
war-cry.

The small boys stop fighting and squabbling for the honour
of manning the Galley's towropes and devote their energies to
getting it on the move. As the Galley moves forward the
waiting lines of torchbearers join in its wake. To the
accompaniment of rockets soaring over the town, Roman
candles spouting coloured lights and stars, and to the martial
music, played alternately by the Brass Band and the Pipes
and Drums, the procession wends its way over the prescribed
route, does the Turning Movement in King Harald Street, and
finally arrives at the head of Victoria Pier. Here, Committee
Men take charge of the Galley, and, while the Viking escort
slowly circles round the doomed ship, the chassis on which it

has been borne is removed and wooden trestles substituted.
Under the direction of the Marshal, other Committee Men form
the main body of the guizers into a huge compact circle. The
stage is set for the final obsequies.

The Band strikes up the Galley Song, and the guizers
and onlookers join in. When the song is finished, the Guizer
Jarl picks up a megaphone and calls for three cheers for the

Builders of the Galley, three cheers for the Torchmakers and again three cheers for Up-Helly-Aa. Scarcely have the cheers died down before the Marshal leaps on to the Galley platform, and, taking over the megaphone, calls for three cheers for the Guizer Jarl. The Jarl acknowledges with a final wave of his battle-axe, and leaps from the poop, a bugle call rings out, and from all sides hundreds of blazing torches hurtle through the air in parabolic curves to land in the waist of the Dragon-ship. For a few moments, only a dull red glow is to be seen inside the Galley, and, then, with a crackle and a roar, the flames leap up and envelop the shrouds and rigging. The Band strikes up The Hardy Norseman, but already a large proportion of the squads has left, and there is only a half-hearted response mostly from the onlookers. For a few moments longer the mast, with the raven banner still fluttering proudly above the inferno below, stands, sways and topples over amid a shower of sparks. The crowd disperses, and high up in Aasgard[56] a smile slowly spreads over the face of the Sun-god.

The squads retire to wash-up and make final adjustments to their dresses, so, while they are doing this, let us look at what has been happening during the last few weeks. Gone are the days when the guizers were entertained in private houses. It simply could not be done, so several groups of householders have clubbed together for the Festival. Halls, hotels and restaurants have been booked, fiddlers and pianists have been engaged to assist the squad fiddlers, and invitations have been sent out to the young ladies, who will dance with the guizers, and to friends of the hosts who will help with the refreshments or simply watch the proceedings. Provision has had to be made to supply refreshments, not only to the guests who may

---

[56]Asgard:—The home of the Norse gods.

number anything from 50 to 100 or more, in each place of entertainment, but probably to over 400 guizers. The bakers have been busy making extra bread, cakes and sausage rolls. The ladies have assembled in the places of entertainment to prepare sandwiches, filling them with generous spreadings of butter and meat or pastes. Tea and coffee and soft drinks are in abundance. No guizer goes hungry on Up-Helly-Aa night.

The day before the Festival, one may encounter in the town various groups of young men carrying bundles under their arms or wearing cloaks from under which protrude legs encased in all sorts of peculiar garments. These are the squads on their way to the photographers where they will don their full guizing dresses and pose or posture for their photographs. The Guizer Jarl has already been photographed by Press photographers in order that his photograph may appear on the official programme and in the Press reports of the Festival.

Let us now make our way to one of the halls where we are welcomed by our hosts. The assembled company sit or stand around discussing the procession, the guizing dresses and the bon-fire. As can be understood the majority of those present are ladies—hostesses fluttering round making sure that everything is in readiness, and young ladies in afternoon dresses. The men in lounge suits are either hosts or friends invited to view what is literally a Passing Show. To the men are allotted the various duties of regulating the number of squads to be admitted at one time, seeing that the guizers receive refreshments and acting as M.Cs. To one of the company is allotted the task of checking off each squad as it arrives—a very necessary proceeding as no host may close down until it is reasonably certain that all the squads have been accounted for.

Round about 10 p.m. the first of the squads is heard approaching and in they come acting their parts or singing a song with words to suit their characterisations. The parade or acting

over, the individual members mix with the guests and start an
'aff-lay'. While the aff-lay is still in progress, one of the
guizers is certain to approach the M.C. with "Whit aboot a
dance?" and soon the ladies are being sedately waltzed around
by masked figures in the magnificent flowing robes of Arab
Sheiks or being madly whirled in a reel in the arms of monkeys
with wildly swinging tails. By the time the dance is over, most
of the squad have been recognised by their partners, and off
come the masks and out come the handkerchiefs to wipe the
sweat from their perspiring faces. At first, the arrival of the
squads is very intermittent so more dances are put on until
another squad puts in an appearance and the first is directed
into the refreshment room accompanied by their lady friends.
Refreshments over, the squad return to the dancing room, give
three cheers for their hosts, don their discarded masks and
accoutrements and sally forth to the next port of call. Often
more squads arrive than the hall can accommodate, and then it
is the duty of the gentlemen in charge to explain the situation
and request the squad to call back later on their rounds. And
so on it goes till 5 or 6 a.m. when the somewhat tired hostesses
enquire how many more have to come, and are relieved to learn
that only one has not been accounted for, and the chances are
that even now this squad is already heard approaching, and,
to judge by their entry, they seem to be as lively as ever. One
more stunt, one more dance, and the whole company join hands
and sing Auld Lang Syne. The older folks, weary but happy,
go off home to a well-earned rest while some of the younger
ones stay on to clear things up a bit, then they, too, leave in
company with weirdly dressed escorts, for it is a curious fact
that love-lorn swains always contrive to finish up where their
sweethearts are, and yet the squads have apparently never lost
their cohesion during the whole night.

The Guizer Jarl's squad is in honour bound to visit every

place of entertainment.   As Vikings, they do not usually indulge in stunts but the Jarl invariably makes a speech in which he thanks the hosts and hostesses for their hospitality, and expresses the gratitude of the Up-Helly-Aa Committee to all who have, once again, made the Up-Helly-Aa Festival such a success.   Innumerable telegrams have reached him on Up-Helly-Aa Day wishing the Festival "Skoal",[57] "Good Luck", "Fine Night", "Bright Torches and Glorious Bon-fire" and so on.   Time was when the Jarl could read all these telegrams in each place of entertainment, but the number grew so large that the services of a lady-typist were enlisted to set them all down on sheets of foolscap, and a copy is left for the hostess to hand round for all who care to read.   These telegrams of greeting come from all over the world from Shetlanders in exile whose minds and hearts turn longingly to The Old Rock on Up-Helly-Aa Night.

The fun on Up-Helly-Aa Night is not exclusively confined to the places of entertainment.   Many of the squads contrive to act their parts as they move from place to place. It is related that some members of a squad, who went out as cats, firmly maintained that the only correct route between one place of entertainment and another was *via* the tops of the walls, and along the tops of all the available walls they went—no mean feat in daylight with a mask on but a somewhat hazardous adventure in the dimly lit lanes at 4 a.m.   Imagine the feelings of a reveller making his way, rather unsteadily, up one of the lanes, when, from overhead, he hears the love-song of an amorous tomcat.   As his eyes turn upwards, they suddenly blink as they rest on two huge cats which, with high-arched backs, are gazing into one another's eyes.   Even as he looks, the courting pair break into an orgy of spitting and scratching

---

[57]Skoal:—Norse toast, literally meaning skull. In Viking times the warriors are reputed to have toasted one another with skulls filled with mead.

followed by a cacophony of caterwauling, and our reveller's astonishment gives way to fear as he senses more huge cats closing in upon him, and all walking erect on their hind legs. With an inward vow never to touch another drop, he takes to his heels, spurred to greater speed by the yowls that break out behind him.

Another squad masquerading as "The Austin Babies" had motor cars which could only be described as libels on the famous Austin Seven. As they passed down the lanes they held hotly contested race-meetings, the winner being the first car to reach the Street. More than one member of this squad maintained that they had almost as much fun in the lanes as they had in the halls. We can leave it to the reader to visualise ten or a dozen cars careering down Queen's Lane, barging first into one wall and then into another and bumping each other indiscriminately. The ludicrousness of this ploy is heightened when one realises that the racing-drivers were babes in their nightdresses with teething teats in the mouths of their baby masks. A stranger, coming suddenly on this scene, might well be excused if he thought he had landed in a lunatic asylum.

Again, the squad of Chanticleers are reputed to have indulged in egg-laying contests in all odd corners of the Street and lanes. The fact that they represented the males of the species was no handicap on Up-Helly-Aa Night.

Well, we have had a good look back at ourselves on many a Yuletide, New'r's Eve and Up-Helly-Aa ; the English and Scottish newspapers have allotted our festivities a considerable amount of newsprint, and the camera news-reels have shewn our revels far and wide, but, now and again, we are privileged to 'see oorsels as ithers see us'. Here are two views taken, one from a West of Scotland newspaper, and the other from an English periodical.

Let us look first at the Scottish one. It must have been written by a leading light of some religious body. He takes a poor view of our culture, and, so slow has been our conversion, that we are inclined to think that one of the Clerical Missionaries of 1877, must have been his ancestor. It must, however, sober our pride to be compared to a 'brake club' of Govan 'ricketties'. Here, then, is his description of our much vaunted Up-Helly-Aa :—

"Lerwick is away up in the Shetland Isles. and we are glad we sent a missionary, or a minister, in that direction some years ago, although we don't see much sign of civilization among the natives as yet. With shields over their arms, tin hats on their heads, feathers and cloaks on their shoulders, white tape crossed over their stockings, and swords in their hands, they get down to the shore, and drag about an old canoe with a wooden sea-serpent at the prow and an ancient helm at the stern. When all is in order, and the camera man in a position to take the official photographs for publication in the pictorials, in rush the descendants of the hardy Norsemen shouting 'Up-Helly-Aa'. The nearest approach we have to anything of this kind is when a brake club with 'ricketties' strikes the town from Govan or Parkhead, and their battle-cry is sometimes varied to 'Up-Helly-O'. As spectacles they are both on a par, except that the one is an innocent pageant of old trouble, and the other a convincing example of present trouble".

One wishes that the writer of this 'report' had gone on to describe more of the action following the 'dragging about of an old canoe', but, as he has failed us, we are fortunate in having an English reporter, who has used his eyes and brains to much better purpose. He writes his eye-witness account thus :—

The Battle of the Guizers.

Annually on or about January 27, there is celebrated at Lerwick, the Capital of the Shetland Isles, the ancient Norse Festival of Up-Helly-Aa.

The proceedings are opened by a sham battle between opposing forces, the combatants being attired in costumes representing those worn by the Vikings, or sea-rovers of old, and carrying swords and shields.

The men taking part in this mimic warfare are called Guizers, and the leader on either side the Guizer Jarl.

One party represents the enemy, the others the defenders of the place, and the whole pageant is intended to portray a Viking foray, such as the 'warriors' ' ancestors were only too familiar with in the days gone by.

After the rout of the invaders, there is a torch-light procession, when songs are sung in honour of the 'victory'.

The proceedings end with the kindling of a huge bon-fire constructed to represent a Norse war-galley.

The subsequent revels are prolonged far into the night, and are celebrated with all manner of old observances, including the solemn drinking of the Shetlanders' national toast 'Health to man and death to the Grey Fish'.

The 'grey fish' is, of course, the whale, which by the way is an 'animal', not a fish.

It is only fitting that this review of the Tar-barrels and Up-Helly-Aa should end with what was, undoubtedly, the most brilliant and spectacular of all Up-Helly-Aa Festivals. It was held on a glorious night which enhanced the picturesque effect of a procession of over 400 guizers. Overhead the Merry Dancers, in hues of green and red, advanced and retired, set and reeled in wild abandon; the torches burned steadily under a pall of lurid smoke which hung still in the air; the innumerable fireworks spouted fountains of coloured flame, or lit the heavens with clusters of glittering stars and trails of fire, all of which added to the brilliance of the scene and provided a vivid setting to the moving lines of torches. Everything went off so well that the Committee could not resist the impulse to have the Turning Movement done twice over, and the Dragon-ship was sent to Valhalla in a perfect blaze of glory.

Hilarity was in the air, and the guizers, hosts and guests made 'whoopee' with feast and dance and laughter till six of the clock next morning.

That was in January, 1939, and, before the year was out, the nation was once more plunged in bloody war. Again the youth of the Town responded to the call, and, again, the sea, the air, the battlefield and the prisoners' camps have claimed their victims.

What of the future? For a period it will be impossible to celebrate the Festival in all its pristine glory. No wood is available for building the Galley, or for making the torch-sticks; old bags might be found to make the torches, but where is the paraffin to come from? The hostesses simply could not produce that backbone of catering—tea and sugar, and, 'fourpence-a-gill' is indeed a 'Thing of the Past'. But, worst of all, where are the clothing coupons to come from, without which no guizing dress can be made? Yes, the immediate future for Up-Helly-Aa is indeed black, but the Sun-god will not wait long for payment of his annual tribute, and, if the cold, clammy fist of bureaucracy closes over-long on the essentials, he will once more stir up the old tar-barrel spirit and inspire the guizers to devise new methods of enforcing their motto, *We Axe For What We Want.*

APPENDIX I.

GUIZER JARLS AND OTHER DATA FROM 1920 TO 1939.

Year	Guizer Jarl	Guizer Jarl's Squad	Galley	Squads	Guizers
1920	Bertie Robertson	No Jarl's squad	No name	13	149
1921	A. P. Hawick	VIKINGS	No name	22	250
1922	Geo. H. Burgess	BALDER (god of Spring)	SIGR (victory)	26	265
1923	John Campbell	FREY (god of Summer)	NJORD (god of wealth, sea and fire)	31	294
1924	Chas. A. Petrie	HEIMDALL (god of the rainbow)	GERDA (personification of Aurora Borealis)	30	286
1925	Laurence Gray	NJORD (god of wealth, sea and fire)	MAURILDI (sea-fire or phosphorescence)	31	297
1926	Chas. A. Manson	HELGELAND VIKINGS	HVITABJORN (White Bear from play by Ibsen)	33	319
1927	Jas. McIntosh	OLAF TRYGGVESON (king of Norway, circa 980 A.D.)	ORMR (serpent)	29	291
1928	Rob. A. Johnson	ULLR (god of archery and Winter)	VEGR (glory)	29	300
1929	P. B. Laurenson	VIKINGS	VALI (god of eternal night)	29	293
1930	P. S. Goodlad	JOM VIKINGS	FRAEGTH (fame)	29	317
1931	J. W. Irvine	JORSALAFARERS (Jerusalem-farers)	IDUN (goddess of Spring)	31	335
1932	Peter Moar	VIKINGS	FRITHR (friendship)	29	322
1933	A. R. M. Mathewson	FRITHIOF (mythological Norse hero)	ELLIDA (Frithiof's dragon-ship)	33	371
1934	Tom Henry	KING SVERRE'S BIRKBEINERS	HUGRO (Sverre's ship)	33	372
1935	John Gear	VIKINGS	SAE-ORN (sea-eagle)	34	422
1936	J. W. P. Angus	VARANGER GUARD (personal bodyguard to Greek empress of Constantinople)	BEYKISUDIN (Southern Beechwood, name of Norse ship)	39	471
1937	Robert Gray	LEIF ERIKSSON (discovered N. America circa 1000 A.D.)	ODUR (personification of the Sun)	33	391
1938	Jas. Anderson	HJALTLANDERS	JOLA-TUNGL (Yule-moon)	31	377
1939	Gilbert Halcrow	ERIK THE RED	VISUND (bison-ox)	32	422

Appendix II.

UP-HELLY-Aa GUIZERS' COMMITTEE.

The Committee is limited to the Guizer Jarl, the Secretary and thirteen Guizers. Vacancies are filled each year by election at the Mass Meeting of the Guizers.

The Guizer Jarl is elected annually. He is usually the senior member of the Committee, holds office for one year, and, on demitting office, automatically becomes Marshal of the Procession for the following year, after which he retires from the Committee unless re-elected.

ORGANISATION OF THE PROCESSION.

The Marshal issues instructions, and is responsible for all details in connection with the Procession.

Party detailed to ensure that the Galley is at the place of assembly on time	4 members
Party detailed to supervise distribution of torches	3 members
Stationed at top of Church Lane to issue vouchers to each squad to draw torches	1 member
Stationed at top of Queen's Lane to check the number of squads which have been issued with torches before forming the Procession. This is necessary to ensure that all squads are present before the Procession moves off	1 member
Detailed to mark the limits of the Turning Movement in King Harald Street	4 members

Detailed to maintain discipline and orderly marching; to every 2 or 3 squads according to the number in each squad   1 member

(These supervisors march between the lines of torch-bearers).

Detailed to lower the mast as the Galley passes below telephone wires   1 man

(The man engaged for this duty must make himself absolutely familiar with where the lines cross the streets).

When the Procession reaches the shore end of Victoria Pier, Committee Men take charge of the Galley, see that it is halted in the correct position and carry out the somewhat intricate job of removing the chassis from under and placing the Galley on trestles in readiness for the burning.

Appendix III.

UP-HELLY-Aa FESTIVAL.

BALANCE SHEET, 1939.

Charge.

To balance carried forward from 1938	£30	2	1
,, subscriptions as per 1939 Collecting Sheet	93	7	6
,, collections at Meetings of Guizers	1	16	9
,, sale of tickets to Country Visitors for admission to Territorial Drill Hall	15	11	0
	£140	17	4

Discharge.

By cost of Fireworks	£4	2	5
,, cost of Galley—materials, wages, insurance etc.	71	12	10
,, cost of 430 Torches—sticks, hessian, paraffin and wages	19	15	2
,, expenses in connection with Territorial Drill Hall— rent, lighting, remuneration of doorkeepers, fiddlers and charwomen scrubbing floor and cleaning hall	10	16	0
,, miscellaneous items of expenditure	11	4	6
	£117	10	11
,, amount on Deposit in The North of Scotland Bank, Ltd.	21	0	0
,, amount on Current Account in The North of Scotland Bank, Ltd.	2	6	5
	£140	17	4

Note:—The amount expended on fireworks is very misleading when one remembers the great displays during the torchlight processions. The amount shewn above was mainly expended on coloured and starred rockets, etc. All other fireworks are gifted by shipping companies and shore institutions which have to keep supplies of maroons and rockets always on hand. These supplies are warranted safe by the Board of Trade for a specified number of years, after which they are renewed. Before being used by the Up-Helly-Aa Committee, all discarded fireworks are examined and passed by qualified experts.

Appendix IV.

The under-noted 'APPEAL' was distributed by the Clerical Missionaries during the Up-Helly-Aa festivities, 1877. It is reputed to have been written by the late J. B. Laurence, the first Editor of the *Shetland News*, and later Curator of the Lerwick Museum. He was famous in his day for his erudite knowledge of Norse lore, and as a waggish wit. The author was once told by an eminent citizen of Lerwick, long since dead, that none of the modern Up-Helly-Aa Bills was comparable with the witty skits which J.B. wrote for Up-Helly-Aa. It is almost certain that he was mainly responsible for the Bill of 1899 which contained so many 'distinctly personal allusions' that the Press refrained from reproducing it. The 'APPEAL' is the only known copy of his wit which has survived.

AN EARNEST APPEAL
FOR THE RESTORATION OF THE ANCIENT
NORSE FAITH OF SHETLAND.

Dear Brother, and still more dearly
      Beloved Sister,

            It is commonly said, and we believe it is now more and more clearly felt that the restoration of the Ancient Simplicity of Faith is the great want of the age. A return to Apostolic simplicity it is said would be a boon beyond price. Could this generation but ascertain whether St. Paul drank his whisky neat, whether St. Peter went to the Haaf, whether the apostolic fishermen wore oilskins, and whether they fished for themselves or for the laird, its happiness would be complete. Alas! what frivolity! We, the Reverend but Humble and Lowly missionaries before you, agree with the principle, but think the change should not be on these trivial points, but on the grand essentials. Hence in our Humble and Lowly but decided opinion the time has come when the Ancient Norse Faith of Shetland in all its sublime and rugged simplicity should be revived with as little delay as the obstinacy of the human mind will admit. What an increase of straightforwardness of character would thereby result? For instance in these degenerate days when we laudably desire to swindle an unsuspecting fellow-mortal we ask him to buy and sell with us, in the course of which we clandestinely appropriate a portion of his vain and transitory earthly possessions; unless indeed, which alas! is far too often the case this sweetly innocent person should entertain the (in his case) wicked desire to do the same with us. Our Norse forefathers, however, favoured no such roundabout procedure. With the beautiful simplicity of Ancient times they merely *took* it from him, with, or perhaps more frequently without his will, thereby saving an immense amount of lying and deceit which may truly be called the crying vices of our times. So also we go solemnly to church on Sunday to make confession of sin, so that we may the more truthfully and conscientiously act up to that confession during the week. But what *we* believe to be sin our Norse forefathers believed to be virtues. and thereby saved themselves untold time and trouble by abstaining from making any darned confession whatever. Did we not say, justly, that the time had arrived for restoring the ancient simplicity of the Norse Faith? Gentle reader will you assist us? Already the signs of the times, to those who can read them, are in our favour. Though the School Board has not yet given its formal adhesion to Odinism, yet, as it has excluded the Bible from the Schools, the rising generation will probably be prepared for the due reception of our, or any other, religious ideas. The clergy will, doubtless, be an obstacle, but if it could be found practicable to enclose them carefully within some space of ground, with convenient access to each other, it is plausibly conjectured that a process of mutual extermination and annihilation will at once be instituted. It may be considered that a Temple will not readily be found, but as the Independent Chapel has, during late years, given forth from its pulpit a variety of opposing and conflicting Faiths, it is hoped that it will not only give us the opportunity of unfolding ours, but may be induced to give us a subscription. And since the word subscription is mentioned, we may state that we have appointed as Treasurer, Mr Ro Bie Sn---dy, a gentleman, who, while lamentably indifferent to the Faith, will nevertheless devote himself with a zealous mind and a single eye to the collection of any trifle that our well-wishers may contribute. The Reverend James Mann has consented to represent Odin and to sit among dark and threatening clouds, provided the clouds be Tobacco smoke, and proceed from his own mouth. It is expected that when Old Bonar realises the price of his Sacred Cow, he will place a thank-offering on our Altar. He has also consented to represent Freya the goddess of Beauty, provided the ladies will look the other way while he is putting on his garments. The present Magistrates and Town Council will be removed beyond the precincts of the Burgh. A Thing will be instituted on the point of Morrison's Pier. It will be presided over by Bl-nd W-ll-m of Br-ss-y since it is known that, like Justitia of old, he will be totally oblivious to any interest but his own. When the weather is unpropitious the Thing will be held in the Museum where the library of books has now petrified into Ogham Stones, unless the stuffed birds do not on this time possess too game a flavour. The inhabitants of the South Kirk Close adjoining the old Church Yard having been observed at early morn to engage solemnly in the Pagan Ceremony of mingling their own ashes with the ashes of their forefathers, will be permitted the privilege of having a perpetual vendetta, or feud, with all other closes pretending to have rights to dry clothes in the said Church-yard. The penalty for kissing a young lady shall be in the first instance to return the stolen property. If, however, the lady be pretty, she shall be held as equally conspiring to tempt the lieges, and, in such aggravated cases, both kisser and kissee shall kneel before the Grand Worthy Chief Templar, who shall without remorse address them for three and a quarter hours on Temperance and Moderation. The Skali, or Hall of the gods, shall be the Established Church, where the gods shall continue to sit round the front gallery as at present. As it is, unfortunately, necessary to propitiate the Evil Principle it is proposed to celebrate the worship of Loki in the U.P. Chapel. Balder having struggled to embrace the views of the Wesleyan connection, and perished in the attempt, a commemorative service will be held in that Chapel weekly, where the Ancient Norse Language of Balderdash will alone be used. As it may be asked why the great goddess Frigga, Odin's queen, is left unhonoured, it may be explained that she vanished, it is supposed, in company with a Plymouth Brother, and so has forfeited her place in the Valhalla.

The first reform necessary is to remove the Free Church bell, not only on account of its barbarous tone, but because it is the very acme of hypocrisy to thunder out so gigantic an invitation to so insignificant a feast. As for us, the Reverend but Humble and Lowly clergymen before you, we are prepared individually to accept the stipend and occupy the pulpit of the first vacant parishes in these isles, or if it be considered more convenient, we are willing to sacrifice our feelings by accepting the stipend and relinquishing the pulpit.

Brethren, assist us; sisters, permit us to salute you with a holy kiss. We may or may not be at the Market Cross next Wednesday evening, at eight o'clock, to explain our views more fully. Nevertheless BE THERE.

FESTIVAL OF UPHELLY 'A, 1877.

NO SURRENDER ! ! !

Remember the eyes of the Vox Populi are upon you.

Appendix V.

THE VIKINGS.

"From the fury of the Norsemen, Good Lord, deliver us."
—*Old English Litany.*

Most people have heard of the Vikings, but comparatively few can tell who they were or what influence they exerted on the political and economic structure of Britain, Europe and Russia from the middle of the 8th to the middle of the 11th centuries. This short treatise is not intended to give a detailed account of the Viking Period, but rather a broad survey mainly based on Professor A. Mawer's book, "The Vikings". The writer has, however, attempted to treat the three groups of Vikings separately, and this can be done only in a somewhat loose manner, as the various groups clash together or go their separate ways throughout the whole Viking Period ; but this arrangement will allow the reader to visualise more readily the spheres of activity of each group.

Prior to the 9th century historians have little on which to base their history beyond fragments of monkish writings and the tales or sagas which were handed down from one generation to another. The term 'Viking', pronounced Vik-ing not Vi-king, means literally 'the dweller by the creek' from the Norse 'vik', a bay or fjord. Some writers maintain that it means people from the district of Vik in South Norway, but Prof. Mawer discounts this derivation from the fact that the word is older than the actual Viking Age, and is found in Anglo-Saxon in the form of 'wicing'.

The causes for the original movement of the Vikings have been debated by several authorities, but it has been found impossible to say with any certainty what particular cause inspired them to leave their native shores and over-run Europe. It is just possible that the narrow cultivated coastal belts and the inshore fishings may not have been able to provide the means of livelihood for their ever increasing population, and they would, perforce, have had to go further afield to obtain the necessaries of life. In this respect they might be compared to the Highland clans, whose glens could not provide sufficient food, and who, therefore, supplemented it by making forays on the fat Lowlands. If this premise be correct, we may then safely surmise that primarily the Vikings were forced abroad not so much by lust of conquest but rather by the necessity of finding the wherewithal for existence and room for expansion. Later, when Harald Haarfagr (Fairhair) obtained supremacy over the numerous small kingdoms in Norway, many of the Norwegian noblemen, rather than submit to Harald's overlordship, migrated to Shetland and Orkney (c.870) which they used as bases for making raids on Harald's long coastline. These raids so exasperated Harald that he fitted out a large expedition, landed at Haraldswick in Unst, Shetland, subdued the Vikings in Shetland, and passed on to do the same in Orkney and the Hebrides. On his return to Norway he formed Orkney and Shetland into an Earldom which was governed by successive Jarls till 1194.

There were three groups of Vikings, all Scandinavian but fairly widely separated—the Norse, the Danes and the Swedes. They were not consolidated till early in the 11th century, when for a short period King Knut (Canute) of Denmark ruled over the whole of Scandinavia and a great part of the British Isles.

The Norse Vikings.

According to Irish legend the Norse settled in Shetland in the 7th century, and forced the Irish monks to move on to Faroe, but even here they got no peace from the Norse pirates. Towards the end of the 8th century the Norse were definitely in Shetland and soon reached Orkney and the Hebrides. It was then a short step to cross the Pentland Firth and over-run Caithness and Sutherland. It is interesting to note that the north part of Scotland became known as Sutherland (Southland) from the fact that it was the land south of Orkney. The Norse Vikings continued their conquests down the west coast of Scotland: the Isle of Man became part of the kingdom of Man and the Hebrides. In 807 Ireland was invaded, and, although parts of the interior were still held by Irish kings, by 834 the conquest was complete. The Norse held undisputed sway till 849, when the Danes made their appearance, and, in spite of fierce resistance by the Norse, established themselves. After a time the Norse and the Danes settled down, and, with varying fortunes, maintained supremacy in Ireland till 1014, when they were defeated by Brian, king of Munster, at Clontarf. Sigtryggr of the Silken Beard was then Viking chief, and he prepared for his fight with Brian by summoning aid from all the Viking settlements in the West and "secured the help of Earl Sigurd of the Orkneys and North Scotland by promise of the kingship of Dublin. Ships came from all parts of the Viking world, from Northumbria, from Man and the Western Islands, from Scotland and the Orkneys, and even from Iceland". Reinforcements from Iceland! What a tribute to the Vikings! First, long-ships must have been despatched to summon assistance, and then the Iceland Vikings had to sail or row their ships some 900 miles over a stretch of turbulent sea to take part in the battle on Good Friday. Both Brian and Sigurd were slain in this battle, but Sigtryggr survived and remained king of Dublin. The supremacy of the Vikings in Ireland was over, and from now on they were gradually absorbed into the national life of the country.

About the end of the 8th century, the Norse Vikings carried their raids down St. George's Channel and round the southwest corner of England, and may have been responsible for the attack on Dorchester which lies near the centre of the south coast.

Both the Norse and the Danes were concerned in the Viking settlements in Northumbria, but the Norse element gained control, and Northumbria was brought into definite connection with the Norse kingdom in Dublin.

If the Irish legend be correct that the Norse were raiding the Faroes by the end of the 7th century, it is probable they knew of Iceland about this period. From Iceland they sailed west to Greenland, and by the year 1000 they had discovered Vinland, the north-east part of North America.

The Danish Vikings.

In the early part of the 9th century, the Danish Vikings held Denmark and the south part of Norway under one rule. From their territorial position it was only natural that their conquests, short of challenging the Norse Vikings, would be directed south towards the Frankish empire, west towards England and east to the Baltic states.

In 810 they plundered the Frisian Islands, and Charlemagne had to strengthen his fleet against them but with small success. Probably owing to trouble over the succession in Denmark, there was a lull in the raids till 833 when they were resumed with greater intensity. By 840 the greater part of Frisia was in their hands, and they were turning their attention to France and England. In 841 they ravaged the valley of the Seine as far as Rouen, and two years later they held Nantes. They sailed up the Garonne and penetrated inland as far as Toulouse. "In 844 Arab historians record their vessels swarming off the coast of Spain like 'dark red sea-birds' but while they effected landings at Lisbon and Cadiz and at Arzilla in Morocco, and capured Seville, with the exception of its citadel, the Mussulman resistance was too stout for them to effect much".

During this period England was attacked in the south and west, and soon afterwards it was the turn of East Anglia. London was ravaged in 842, and by 851 we find them wintering in Thanet. "The size and importance of these attacks may be gauged from the fact that in this year (851) a fleet of some 350 Danish ships sailed up the Thames". By 855 the Danish Vikings had arrived at much the same position in the south of England as had the Norse Vikings in Ireland, that is to say they had come to stay and were carrying on their trade and forays from their new settlements. By 871 the Danes had over-run Mercia and Wessex, and London was forced to pay ransom. It was about this time that King Alfred began his struggle against the Danes with varying success, but it was almost the end of the century before he gained mastery, and the Danes withdrew, those who had no cattle returning to France, while those who had the wherewithal to stock farms joined up with East Anglian and Northumbrian Danes.

The raids on England continued, off and on, till the closing years of the 10th century, when the second period of invasion took place and lasted till 1016, which, with Knut king of all England, marks the end of the Danish and Norse Periods in English history; but it was far from the end of Viking influence, as great tracts of England from Northumbria downwards had been settled by the Vikings and their descendants. Two interesting events occurred during the second period of invasion. First, in 994 the Norse Vikings under Olaf Tryggvason sailed up the Thames with 490 ships and laid siege to London. The siege was not successful, but, even so, Ethelred deemed it prudent to come to terms with Olaf, and paid him sixteen thousand pounds to desist from further attacks. The second interesting fact is that during a period of little more than twenty years the English paid the equivalent of about half-a-million sterling to the Vikings in the vain hope of buying off their attacks. These payments became known as Danegeld.

Contemporary with the invasion of England, the Danes kept up continuous attacks on the Frankish empire. They had more or less permanent quarters all along the coast from the Scheldt to Bordeaux. The Low Countries were in their possession and they over-ran France and Germany. They raided Spain and set off to capture Rome, captured Pisa and Luna, but, according to Scandinavian tradition, they mistook Luna for Rome, so went no further south. By this voyage "the Vikings had now almost encircled Europe with their attacks for it was in the year 865 that the Swedish Rhôs (Russians) laid siege to Constantinople". It is during this period (c.881) that their conquests have a striking likeness to the Allied armies' advance during 1944/45, "After their defeat at Saucourt the main body of the Danes made their way to Elsloo on the Meuse when they ravaged the Meuse, Rhine and Moselle districts plundering Cologne, Bonn, Coblentz, Aachen, Treves and Metz". Another of their exploits was in 885 when they sailed up the Seine to Paris with 30,000 men and a fleet of 700 ships. Before Paris they found that the river bridges had been fortified but for a time the position of Paris was desperate. The Vikings, however, were determined to raid beyond Paris, and, as the bridges were closed to them, they dragged many of their ships two miles overland, and continued their forays on the upper reaches of the Seine.

The Franks were unable to dislodge them from the Lower Seine district, and in 911 Charles granted Rollo, the Viking chief, that portion of France which later became known as Normandy. According to Norse tradition, Rollo was the son of Rögnvaldr, earl of Möre, and was exiled by Harald Haarfagr in Norway. He became the first Duke of Normandy, and forbear of William the Conqueror, and thus one of the ancestors of the British Royal Family. It may be of interest to record that he was near kinsman to the early Earls of Orkney and Shetland.

There is not much reliable evidence of the activities of the Danish Vikings in the Baltic, but the fact that several towns on its southern coast bear Scandinavian names points to extensive Viking settlements. About 830 a Danish fleet captured a city of the Slavs, and in 835 we hear of the Swedish Vikings trying to reconquer Kurland in the Gulf

of Riga which had been previously under their rule but had fallen a
prey to the Danish Vikings.

The Swedish Vikings.

From time to time both Norse and Danish Vikings made their
appearance in the Baltic, but, again from their geographical position,
it was the Swedish Vikings who were mainly responsible for the conquest
of this territory. They levied tribute on the Finns, Tartars and Slavs
inhabiting the forest regions round Lake Ilmen, and between Lake
Ladoga and the upper reaches of the Dnieper. "The chief work of the
Swedes was however to be done in lands yet further south, in the heart
of the modern empire of Russia in Europe". It will come as a
surprise to most people to learn that the Swedish Vikings were
responsible for giving Russia its name. For many years Slav patriots
contested this but the evidence proved too strong, and there is now
general agreement that the Swedes did provide the name. Prof. Mawer
goes very fully into this subject, and this short extract will give a good
idea how the proofs were arrived at. "The name 'Rus' is Slavonic,
'Rhôs' the Greek and 'Rûs' the Arabic form of the Finnish name for
Sweden, viz., Ruotsi . . . The Finns had early come into relation
with the Swedes . . . and when the Swedes settled in Russia, the
Finns applied the same term to the new colonists and the term came
to be adopted later into the various Slavonic dialects".

The Swedish Vikings carried on an extensive trade with the East
by way of the east of the Caspian and along the valley of the Volga.
This is proved by the number of Arabic coins found in Sweden, and
the dates thereon place the period between 850 and 1000. "The
Vikings were all-powerful in Western and Southern Russia during the
greater part of the two centuries, carrying on an extensive trade with
the East, establishing Novgorod, 'the new town', on the Volga under
the name Holmgarthr and founding a dynasty which ruled in Kiev and
became a considerable power in eastern Europe, negotiating on terms of
equality with the Byzantine emperors". The Swedish Vikings also
entered the service of the emperor of Constantinople, and from there
they visited all parts of the Mediterranean.

The Viking Ships.

While to a great extent the history of the Vikings is based on the
sagas and the not always too accurate monkish writings, we are on surer

ground with regard to their ships, for not only do the sagas describe them but we have the remains of actual ships which have been discovered. It was not an uncommon custom among the Vikings to bury their dead in the ships which had carried them on their lawful and unlawful occasions during their lifetimes. After the ship in which the body lay in state had been placed in the desired locality, a how or mound was erected over it, and it was due to this custom that we have first-hand information about their construction. Prof Mawer gives this account. "The two most famous are those of Gokstad and Oseberg, both found on the shores of Christiania (Oslo) Fjord. The Gokstad vessel is of oak, clinker-built, with seats for sixteen pairs of rowers, and is 78 feet long and 16 feet broad amidships. It dates from about 900, and in form and workmanship is not surpassed by modern vessels of a similar kind. There is a mast for a single sail, and the rudder, as always in these days, is on the starboard side. The gunwale was decorated with a series of shields painted alternately black and gold. The appearance of the vessel when fully equipped can perhaps best be judged from the pictures of Viking ships to be seen in the Bayeux tapestry. There we may note the parti-coloured sail with its variegated stripes, and the rich carving of stem and stern. These magnificent sails were a source of much pride to their possessors, and the story is told of Sigurd Jerusalem-farer that on his way home from Jerusalem to Constantinople he lay for half-a-month off Cape Malea, waiting for a side wind, so that his sails might be set lengthwise along the ship and so be better seen by those standing on the shore as he sailed up to Constantinople. The stem often ended in a dragon's head done over with gold, whilst the stern was frequently shaped like a dragon's tail, so that the vessel itself was often called a dragon. The Oseberg ship is of a different type. The gunwale is lower and the whole vessel is flatter and broader. It is used as the grave-chamber of a woman, and the whole appearance of the vessel, including its richly carved stem, indicates that it was used in calm waters for peaceful purposes . . . In the last years of the Viking period ships increased greatly both in size and number. Olaf Tryggvason's vessel, the *Long Serpent,* in which he fought his last fight at Svoldr, had thirty benches of oars, while Cnut (Canute) the Great had one with sixty pairs of oars. This same king went with a fleet of some fourteen hundred vessels to the conquest of Norway".

Prof. Mawer is mistaken when he states that the Gokstad Ship had 'seats for sixteen pairs of rowers'. N. Nicolaysen, who was

President of the Norwegian Antiquarian Society, and was responsible for the excavation in 1880 of the Gokstad Viking Ship, gives the number of benches as sixteen, but, as there were thirtytwo shields on either side of the ship, the rowers must have been sixtyfour. Nicolaysen computes the total crew at about seventy.

Nicolaysen also gives a description of the *Long Serpent*, built in 999, which, he says, had a keel of 34.82 metres (113 feet) and most likely thirtyfour benches which, with three men to each oar, would give, at least, 204 oarsmen, while "were there, as is said, 8 men to each halfdivision (i.e. two halfdivisions to each bench) the whole crew would amount to 524, exclusive of those in the prow and in the stern".

As already noted, the Vikings sailed up the Seine in 885, approximately the same date as the Gokstad ship. Thirty thousand men were carried in 700 ships, which gives an average of over 40 men to each ship exclusive of stores and equipment. It might be argued that a proportion of this immense army kept pace with the ships on the river banks, but after the defeat of the Danes by the Bretons in 888 and again by the Franks in 891, followed by a famine in 892, the whole of the remnants of the army estimated at ten to fifteen thousand together with their horses, war equipment and stores, crossed to England in one passage in about 250 ships, which gives an average of 40 to 60 men to each ship.

Their trading-ships must have been of much the same shape and build, as the following incident makes clear :—

"The story of the escape of Hárek of Thjotta through Copenhagen Sound after the battle of Helgeäa in 1018 illustrates the difference between a trading-ship and a ship of war. Hárek struck sail and mast, took down the vane, stretched a grey tent-cloth over the ship's sides, and left only a few rowers fore and aft. The rest of the crew were bidden lie flat so that they might not be seen, with the result that the Danes mistook Hárek's war-galley for a trading-vessel laden with herrings or salt and let it pass unchallenged".

Barbarities.

The short prayer from the old English litany which appears as a heading to this treatise gives a fairly accurate clue to one side of the Viking character. The Vikings were undoubtedly cruel, but as cruelty appears to have been part of their creed, they suffered from no qualms of conscience. Adam of Bremen has put it on record that the Danes can weep neither for their sins nor for their dead. It is recorded that after the fight between the Norse and the Danes in Ireland "the Danes cooked their food on spits stuck in the bodies of their fallen foes, and when asked (by the Irish) why they did anything so hateful, the answer came 'Why not? if the other side had been victorious they would have done the same with us'. The custom of cutting the blood-eagle (i.e. cutting the ribs in the shape of an eagle and pulling the lungs through the opening) was a well-known form of vengeance taken on the slayer of one's father if captured in battle".

A common form of dealing with one's enemies was to catch them in their houses at night, tie the doors and burn the house down. Still another was to put out the eyes of potential rivals, and to illustrate how this practice was a recognised one, we hear of St. Magnus pleading with his murderer, Hakon, to blind him and keep him captive in a dungeon rather than that Hakon should be tainted with blood-guiltiness. One of their most loathsome cruelties was tossing children on the point of a spear, and the "Viking leader who discouraged the custom was nicknamed 'barnakarl', i.e., children's friend".

Many more instances of cruelties could be given, but enough have been noted to illustrate this barbarous trait in the Vikings' make-up. This trait also permeated their poetry. "Yet more interesting perhaps is the old lay preserved to us, the Song of the Valkyries, who that same day were seen in Caithness riding twelve together to a bower where they set up a loom of which men's heads were the weights, men's entrails the warp and the woof, while a sword was the shuttle and the reels were arrows. They wove the web of war and foretold the fate of King Sigtryggr and Earl Sigurd as well as the sharp sorrow which would befall the Irish". This portent refers to the battle of Clontarf.

It would be wrong to assume from the foregoing that barbaric cruelties and customs were solely confined to the Vikings. Their war-like character and their vast conquests were mainly responsible for propagating their reputation for barbarism, but, during the Viking Period and long after, barbarous cruelties were by no means unknown among nations who had professedly adopted Christianity. For instance the Vikings could not have excelled the Spanish Inquisition in the refinements of the tortures executed in the name of the Church, the acts of vengeance in England and Scotland, in which latter country we

have the infamous Rape of Buchan, and even now after 2000 years
of Christian teaching we have the most terrible cruelties of all, the
sadistic horrors of the Nazi Concentration Camps.[58]

Civilisation, Trade and Culture.

In contrast to the primitive barbarism of the Vikings we find that
they had developed a business ability and culture which placed them
in a higher degree of civilisation than many of their European neighbours.
Their conquests demonstrate that their tactical skill in war was high,
and one does not require to comment on their seamanship without which
there could have been no Viking Period.

As traders they must have excelled, for if ever trade followed the
flag, the Viking merchant ships were hard on the heels of the long-ships.
As Prof. Mawer remarks "the line of division between the merchant
and the Viking was a very thin one, and more than once we read how,
when merchants went on a trading expedition, they arranged a truce
until their business was concluded and then treated each other as
enemies". The Viking exports were chiefly furs, horses, wool and fish,
and they imported luxuries such as clothing and ornaments. Another
lucrative side of their trading was in captives, girls, young women, boys
and prisoners of war. Prof. Mawer relates an incident which
illustrates the international character of this traffic:—

"On a certain occasion a wealthy merchant named Gille (the
name is Celtic), surnamed the Russian because of his many journeys
to that country, set up his booth in the market and received a visit from
the Icelander Höskuldr who was anxious to buy a female slave. Gille

---

[58]The following extracts are taken from "A History of the Vikings",
by T. D. Hendrick, M.A. Mr Hendrick is one of the greatest authorities
on the Viking Period, and is in charge of English and Medieval Antiquities,
British Museum.

Page 12.—"As buccaneers, thieves and murderers . . . . they were no
worse than other robbers and pillagers of history either before their day
or long after it, yet it is an idle and dishonest task to attempt to defend
them against the charge of plundering and massacre".

Page 37.—"For the Viking, whatever he may have done abroad, ...
must be seen against a cultural background that deserves respect. He
came of a people who were endowed with considerable aesthetic sensibility
and who were in some trades, such as shipbuilding and ironwork, craftsmen
of more than ordinary skill. Therefore, though it is profitless to look for
such a thing as a typical Viking, since throughout the whole of their
history the Vikings were exactly what their circumstances made them.
robbers, colonists and traders, yet it is a nearer approach to the truth to
believe that they were an orderly and sensible civilised folk than that
they were bloody and destructive brutes".

drew back a curtain dividing off the inner part of the tent and shewed Höskuldr twelve female slaves. Höskuldr bought one and she proved to be an Irish king's daughter who had been made captive by Viking raiders".

The Vikings were guilty of two besetting sins—immoderate love of wine and women. On many occasions their drinking bouts were the cause of fights to the death among close friends, and, like Jack Tar, they had wives in every port, albeit they were, in the main, staunch to their legal spouses. On the other hand, wandering as they did from country to country, polygamy seems to have been the rule, at least among the leaders.

When not engaged in trade and war which appear to have been their chief occupations, they led the lives of country gentlemen, farming their lands, raising stock and administering their estates. They admitted no inequality of rank, and the daughter of a jarl might marry the poorest of the Vikings without loss of status. While this was so, they recognised the necessity for leaders, and to them the Viking gave his loyalty, or, as they put it, 'became their man'. Their houses were built of wood with the hearth in the middle of the floor, the smoke from the fire finding its way as best it could through the turf-covered roof.

The Vikings were much addicted to personal ornaments and dress, in the fashioning and designing of which they attained high artistic skill. At one time it was assumed that their ornaments were simply the results of their plunderings, but investigation has shewn that most of them were made in Scandinavia. Their sculptured stones also show the same high degree of artistic development, and the carving on their furniture often portrayed scenes of heroic deeds.

Religion.

Like their history, very little is known of the religious customs of the early Norse, but the Icelandic Eddas and Sagas give us a fair idea of the religious faiths as practised by them. They had their major and minor gods and goddesses, who held sway over earth, sea, the elements and practically every phase of human life. The gods lived in Åsgard (home of the gods), had the human attributes of love, marriage, bearing of children, and death, and were subject to expulsion from Åsgard, but could be re-instated.

Chief among the gods was Odin, the all-wise, whose throne was in Valhalla (hall of the dead), to which all warriors hoped to be

admitted.   Thor, the god of thunder, was probably the strongest of
all the gods, and was deemed to be Friend of Men.   Tíw whose
symbol was a sword, was the god of war.   These three were the
mighty gods, and, after them, came the inferior gods and goddesses,
but, as this is not a treatise on Norse mythology, we must leave
mythology alone, and deal with the attitude of the Vikings in their
relations with their celestial lords.   Before doing this, however, it is of
interest to know that all the authorities agree that the chief gods,
usually twelve in number, can be identified with the same gods
acknowledged by the Greeks, Romans and even the Hindus, the
difference being only in the conception of the gods as influenced by
geographical position.

If proof were needed to connect the old Norse religion with that
of India, we have only to compare the burial rites as practised by the
Vikings and the Hindus.   A pamphlet giving an eye-witness account
of "the incremation of the dead body of a Norse chief", written in
the early part of the Tenth Century,[59] gives minute details of the last
rites, on which the modern conception of the Up-Helly-Aa procession
and bon-fire is mainly based.

The account tells how the dead Chief, arrayed in garments of
gold-worked cloth and jewels, is laid-in-state on a richly adorned bed
aboard his long-ship, which had been drawn up on the shores of the
Volga.   Along with the Chief, were placed the bodies of two
pack-horses, two oxen, a cock and a hen, and a dog.   The dead
Chief's weapons were laid by his side, and a supply of strong drinks
and victuals provided for his journey to Valhalla.   Last of all, a
maiden, who had volunteered to accompany her dead master, was
slain and laid by the side of her late lord.   The brushwood, which had
been placed under the ship, was then set alight by the Chief's nearest
relative, and the last rites had been performed.

Is the foregoing brief account of the funeral rites of a Viking
Chief not paralleled by the funeral pyre and sutteeism practised upon
the widows and concubines of the Hindu maharajahs, prior to 1829,
when the British Government abolished it?

---

[59]*Description* by Ahmed Ibn-Fozlan (an Eye-Witness) of the
Ceremonies Attending the *Incremation* of the *Dead Body* of a *Norse
Chief*, written in the early part of the Tenth Century.   Translated from
Holmboe's Danish Version of the Arabic Original, with Notes of the Origin
of Cremation, and its Continuance by Joseph Anderson, Keeper of the
Museum, Edinburgh.

So far as the public worship of the gods is concerned, it is conjectured that the first temples were open spaces in the forests. At a later period "according to these descriptions (old Icelandic literature), the Scandinavian temple was a right-angled, oblong building, consisting of two unpartitioned chambers, a larger and a smaller, with a semi-circular apse visible from the outside, and probably containing the sacred requisites used for worship. The building material was wood probably with ornamental carving . . . . A building 130 yards long and 65 broad was considered unusual in Iceland. The building was enclosed, its walls provided with loopholes, it had an open roof, and was adorned with wall-hangings; occasionally the walls were further ornamented with precious metals. On the door hung a ring. Within the temple doors were pillars supporting the structure; in the middle of the longer northern wall stood a seat of honour for the guardian of the temple, with representations of the gods on its posts; lower benches ran along the shorter side-walls; in the semi-circular apse probably stood images of the gods . . . . In the temple the images of several gods stood together. In front of them was the altar covered with iron, on which burned the sacred never-dying fire. There, too, lay an unclosed ring, with which all oaths were sworn. The priest had to dip it into the blood of the animal sacrificed, and apparently wore it round his neck at all festive assemblies as a symbol of dependence upon divine favour. There was besides on the altar a great copper vessel of blood, and a small brush with which to smear the blood upon the altar, and to sprinkle those who assisted at the sacrifice . . . . As a rule there was a larger or smaller wood outside the building, with a sacred sacrificial well into which the bodies of the victims were lowered".

The foregoing description of a Norse temple is taken from "Northern Mythology", by Prof. D. Fredrich Kauffmann. as translated by M. Steele Smith, Cambridge University. It gives a better picture of a temple than the writer could possibly hope to do. and for the same reason he again quotes Kauffman at length on the three great annual festivals :—

"Thrice a year the people of the district came together in order to attend the great sacrificial festivals in the temple. At WINTER-NIGHT (about the middle of October) sacrifices were offered for a good season; at MID-WINTER (the end of January) the Yuletide festival was kept, when for three days sacrifices were offered for peace

and fertility; at BEGINNING OF SUMMER (the middle of April) the
people petitioned for good luck and victory in the undertakings of the
coming summer. The sacrifices were intended to gain the gods' favour
and appease their wrath. The offerer hoped to avert injury at the
hands of the invisible powers and to reap personal advantage. Sacrifice
is offered by man to the gods in expectation of benefits from them in
return; a human life is sacrificed to them in order that they shall spare
the survivors. It was the occasion of special rejoicing if the god
shewed a sign that the sacrifice was acceptable : if, for instance, Odin's
ravens appeared in sight.

"The sacrifices as a rule involved the shedding of blood: the
priest had to slaughter oxen, horses, sheep, swine, and collect the
blood in the vessel set apart for the purpose. Thereupon a fire was
kindled in the middle of the temple, the flesh cooked in cauldrons, the
broth and the meat consumed together . . . . One of the Christian
missionaries narrates that in the great sacrificial grove of Upsala he saw
seventy-two carcases of dogs, horses and men hanging on the trees as
a propitiation of the gods. Human sacrifices were frequent. Saxa
Grammaticus relates that once a Norse king, when in great straits, even
sacrificed his two brave sons in order to purchase victory for his country
from the gods of war with the blood of his own kin. The people were
wont to tarry together at the religious feasts, the expenses of which
were defrayed by the priest from the temple revenues; or, in other
cases (e.g., in Norway), everything needed for the feast had to be
brought by the individuals. Hogsheads of beer and mead were
emptied, after the drinking horn had been consecrated in the fire, in
draughts of grateful remembrance (called 'minne') first to Odin for
victory and might, and afterwards to other gods and departed relatives.
This was also the occasion for taking vows accompanied by solemn
recitation and harp-playing, for receiving divine consecration in serious
resolves and for deepening and strengthening one's purpose in life".

Take away the sacrifices and the images, and we find that the
old Norse faith was not so very much different from what we practise
to-day, and it was for this very reason that the change from paganism
to Christianity was the more easily assimilated by the Norse   True,
it was a long process, stretching over most of the Viking Period,
and would probably have taken longer had it not been for the rough
and ready and, oftimes, harsh methods of conversion adopted by Olaf

Tryggvason and, after him, by St. Olaf, the most fervid of all the kings of Norway in the conversion of his people, towards the end of the Ninth and the beginning of the Tenth Centuries.

During the long period of conversion, the old and the new faiths were practised side by side, and, on more than one occasion, we find instances of men, who were apparently devout Christians, commending themselves to the gods when their end drew near. The new faith, too, sat lightly on the shoulders of many of the chiefs, and, when serious business or trouble was brewing, we find them soliciting the old gods for help. It is related that Helgé the Lean was a Christian but called on Thor in the hour of need. Prof. Mawer writes: "Leaders freely accepted baptism—often more than once—and even confirmation as part of a diplomatic bargain, while their profession of Christianity made no difference to their Viking way of life".

In none of the authorities examined by the writer, can any reference to Fire Worship, as such, be found. NJORD was the god of fire, and to him were supplications and sacrifices made, not to the living flame. The present-day news-writers have fallen into the error of associating the Up-Helly-Aa celebrations with Fire Worship, whereas, the institution of the pageant depicting the funeral rites of a Viking Jarl is definitely a re-enactment of an historical fact.

This does not explain, however, the connection between the original bonfire or tar-barrel and an ancient Norse festival. Up-Helly-Aa does coincide with the date of the second of the great sacrificial feasts, and the burning of the Clavie at Burghead and the burning of the tar-barrel in Shetland also coincide with this date. both events being traditionally associated with the Vikings. Religious beliefs, superstitions, if you will, are so deeply rooted in human nature that we, professing Christians, still carry on our persons, amulets. lucky stones and swastikas—not so popular since 1939—treasure found horse-shoes, pick up iron nails, are careful not to spill salt, refuse to walk under ladders or look at the new moon through glass; so why should not some instinctive chord of remembrance of the sacrificial fire of the greatest of the sacrificial feasts of our forefathers not remain with us through the ages, and, when MID-WINTER comes. compel us, not knowing why, to light the fires of sacrifice to our ancestral gods?

INDEX.